Alice

S E R I E S

A life-changing encounter
with God's Word from the books of

LEVITICUS &
NUMBERS

D1509980

Discipleship Inside Out®

NAVPRESS

Discipleship Inside Out®

NavPress is the publishing ministry of The Navigators, an international Christian organization and leader in personal spiritual development. NavPress is committed to helping people grow spiritually and enjoy lives of meaning and hope through personal and group resources that are biblically rooted, culturally relevant, and highly practical.

**For a free catalog go to www.NavPress.com
or call 1.800.366.7788 in the United States or 1.800.839.4769 in Canada.**

1 2 3 4 5 6 7 8 / 20 19 18 17 16 15 14

203.59

CONTENTS

HOW TO USE THIS GUIDE

Along with all the volumes in the LIFECHANGE series of Bible studies, this guide to Leviticus and Numbers shares common goals:

1. To provide you with a firm foundation of understanding, plus a thirst to return to Leviticus and Numbers throughout your life.

2. To give you study patterns and skills that help you explore every part of the Bible.

3. To offer you historical background, word definitions, and explanation notes to aid your study.

4. To help you grasp as a whole the message of both Leviticus and Numbers.

5. To teach you how to let God's Word transform you into Christ's image.

As you begin

This guide includes twelve lessons, which will take you chapter by chapter through all of Leviticus and Numbers. Each lesson is designed to take from one to two hours of preparation to complete on your own. To benefit most from this time, here's a good way to begin your work on each lesson:

1. Pray for God's help to keep you mentally alert and spiritually sensitive.

2. Read attentively through the entire passage mentioned in the lesson's title. (You may want to read the passage from two or more Bible versions—perhaps at least once from a more literal translation such as the New International Version, English Standard Version, New American Standard Bible, or New King James Version, and once more in a paraphrase such as The Message or the New Living Translation.) Do your reading in an environment that's as free as possible from distractions. Allow your mind and heart to meditate on these words you encounter, words which are God's personal gift to you and to all His people.

After reading the passage, you're ready to dive into the numbered questions in this study which make up the main portion of each lesson. Each of these questions is followed by blank space for writing your answers. (This act of writing your answers helps clarify your thinking and stimulates your mental engagement with the passage, as well as your later recall.) Use extra paper or a notebook if the space for recording your answers seems too cramped. Continue through the questions in numbered order. If any question seems too difficult or unclear, just skip it and go on to the next.

Each of these questions will typically direct you back to Leviticus or Numbers to look again at a certain portion of the assigned passage for that lesson. (At this point be sure to use a more literal Bible translation, rather than a paraphrase.)

As you look closer at this passage, it's helpful to approach it in this progression:

Observe. What does the passage actually *say?* Ask God to help you see it clearly. Notice everything that's there.

Interpret. What does the passage *mean?* Ask God to help you understand. And remember that any passage's meaning is fundamentally determined by its *context.* So stay alert to all you'll see about the setting and background of Leviticus and Numbers, and keep thinking of these books as a whole while you proceed through them chapter by chapter. You'll be progressively building up your insights and familiarity with what they're all about.

Apply. Keep asking yourself, *How does this truth affect my life?* (Pray for God's help as you examine yourself in light of that truth, and in light of His purpose for each passage.)

Try to consciously follow all three of these approaches as you shape your written answer to each question in the lesson.

The extras

In addition to the regular numbered questions you see in this study, each lesson also offers several "optional" questions or suggestions that appear in the margins. All of these will appear under one of three headings:

Optional Application. These are suggested options for application. Consider these with prayerful sensitivity to the Lord's guidance.

For Thought and Discussion. Many of these questions address various ethical issues and other biblical principles that lead to a wide range of implications. They tend to be particularly suited for group discussions.

For Further Study. These often include cross-references to other parts of the Bible that shed light on a topic in the lesson, plus questions that delve deeper into the passage.

(For additional help for more effective Bible study, refer to the "Study Aids" section on page 135.)

Changing your life

Don't let your study become an exercise in knowledge alone. Treat the passage as *God's* Word, and stay in dialogue with Him as you study. Pray, "Lord, what do You want me to notice here?" "Father, why is this true?" "Lord, how does my life measure up to this?"

Let biblical truth sink into your inner convictions so you'll increasingly be able to act on this truth as a natural way of living.

At times you may want to consider memorizing a certain verse or passage you come across in your study, one that particularly challenges or encourages you. To help with that, write down the words on a card to keep with you, and set aside a few minutes each day to think about the passage. Recite it to yourself repeatedly, always thinking about its meaning. Return to it as often as you can, for a brief review. You'll soon find the words coming to mind spontaneously, and they'll begin to affect your motives and actions.

For group study

Exploring Scripture together in a group is especially valuable for the encouragement, support, and accountability it provides as you seek to apply God's Word to your life. Together you can listen jointly for God's guidance, pray for each other, help one another resist temptation, and share the spiritual principles you're learning to put into practice. Together you affirm that growing in faith, hope, and love is important and that *you need each other* in the process.

A group of four to ten people allows for the closest understanding of each other and the richest discussions in Bible study, but you can adapt this guide for other sized groups. It will suit a wide range of group types, such as home Bible studies, growth groups, youth groups, and church classes. Both new and mature Christians will benefit from the study, regardless of their previous experience in Bible study.

Aim for a positive atmosphere of acceptance, honesty, and openness. In your first meeting, candidly explore everyone's expectations and goals for your time together.

A typical schedule for group study is to take one lesson per week, but feel free to split lessons if you want to discuss them more thoroughly. Or, omit some questions in a lesson if your preparation or discussion time is limited. (You can always return to this guide later for further study on your own.)

When you come together, you probably won't have time to discuss all the questions in the lesson, so it's helpful to choose ahead of time the ones you want to make sure to cover thoroughly. This is one of the main responsibilities that a group leader typically assumes.

Each lesson in this guide ends with a section called "For the Group." It gives advice for that particular lesson on how to focus the discussion, how to apply the lesson to daily life, and so on. Reading each lesson's "For the Group" section ahead of time can help the leader be more effective in guiding the group.

You'll get the greatest benefit from your time together if each group member also prepares ahead of time by writing out their answers to each question in the lesson. The private reflection and prayer that this preparation can stimulate will be especially important in helping everyone discern how God wants you to apply each lesson to your daily life.

There are many ways to structure the group meeting, and in fact you may want to vary your routine occasionally to help keep things fresh.

Here are some of the elements you can consider including as you come together for each lesson:

Pray together. It's good to pause for prayer as you begin your time together, as well as to incorporate a later, more extensive time of prayer for each other after you've had time to share personal needs and prayer requests (you may want to write these down in a notebook). When you begin with prayer, it's worthwhile and honoring to God to ask especially for His Holy Spirit's guidance of your time together.

Worship. Some groups like to sing together and worship God with prayers of praise.

Review. You may want to take time to discuss what difference the previous week's lesson has made in your life, as well as recall the major emphasis you discovered in the passage for that week.

Read the passage aloud. Once you're ready to focus attention together on the assigned Scripture passage in this week's lesson, read it aloud. (One person could do this, or the reading could be shared.)

Open up for lingering questions. Allow time for the group members to mention anything in the passage that they may have particular questions about.

Summarize the passage. Have one or two persons offer a summary of what the passage tells us about.

Discuss. This will be the heart of your time together and will likely take the biggest portion of your time. Focus on the questions you see as the most important and most helpful. Allow and encourage everyone to be part of the discussion on each question. You may want to take written notes as the discussion proceeds. Ask follow-up questions to sharpen your attention and to deepen your understanding of what you discuss. You may want to give special attention to the questions in the margin under the heading "For Thought and Discussion."

Encourage further personal study. You can find more opportunities for exploring this lesson's themes and issues under the marginal heading "For Further Study" throughout the lesson. You can also pursue some of these together during your group time.

Focus on application. Look especially at the "Optional Application" listed in the margins throughout the lesson. Keep encouraging one another in the continual work of adjusting our lives to the truths God gives us in Scripture.

Summarize your discoveries. You may want to read aloud through the passage one last time together, using this opportunity to solidify your understanding and appreciation of it and to clarify how the Lord is speaking to you through it.

Look ahead. Glance together at the questions in the next lesson, to see what's coming next.

Give thanks to God. It's good to end your time together by pausing to express gratitude to God for His Word and for the work of His Spirit in your minds and hearts during your time together.

THE BOOK OF LEVITICUS

Blood and Fire, Grace and Law

The book of Leviticus is not an easy one for believers today to study.

"No book in the Old Testament presents a greater challenge to the modern reader than Leviticus, and imagination is required to picture the ceremonies and rites that form the bulk of the book. However, it is important to try to understand the rituals in Leviticus for two reasons.

"First, rituals enshrine, express, and teach those values and ideas that a society holds most dear. By analyzing the ceremonies described in Leviticus, we can learn about what was most important to the Old Testament Israelites.

"Second, these same ideas are foundational for the New Testament writers. Particularly the concepts of sin, sacrifice, and atonement found in Leviticus are used in the New Testament to interpret the death of Christ."[1]

Studying Leviticus takes diligence and concentration, but that effort yields a uniquely satisfying reward.

The Setting of Leviticus

The events recorded in Leviticus took place when the Israelites, having left Egypt, were encamped before Mount Sinai. Here they stayed for about a year. "During that time Moses spent eighty days on the mountain with God. Then the people of Israel, at Moses' instruction, built the wilderness tabernacle. During this year Moses organized the nation, built up the army, established courts and laws, and ordered formal worship. It was a busy year."[2]

It was also a time when God graciously revealed Himself, to the lasting benefit of His people.

"Leviticus is . . . more than a description of past historical events and more than a collection of dated laws. It tells us about God's character and will, which found expression in his dealings with Israel and in the laws he gave them. Those who believe that God the Lord 'is the same yesterday and today and for ever' may look to the book's theology for insights that are still valid and relevant."[3]

Learning from Leviticus Today

Leviticus helps believers today especially in their understanding of holiness, worship, and atonement for sin—as well as in many other ways. And its lessons come to us in a rich and profound context.

"Though at first glance the book [of Leviticus] looks like an accumulation of laws, this impression is inaccurate. Leviticus is really part of the great history of Israel's journey from Egypt to the promised land. The law-giving was one of the most important events in this story.

"In interpreting Leviticus, and especially in seeking to apply it to the modern situation, the historical context of the laws should be borne in mind. They are not timeless universal precepts such as are found in the book of Proverbs. The laws of Leviticus were revealed to the covenant nation at a particular phase of their history. They were designed to mold Israel into a holy people in a particular historical environment. Though God's holiness is unchanging, its expression may vary from age to age."[4]

Traditionally, Moses is viewed as the author of the Pentateuch—the first five Old Testament books, including Leviticus. However, there are indications in the text of editing and updating done by others after the time of Moses.

1. *New Geneva Study Bible* (Nashville: Thomas Nelson, 1995), introduction to Leviticus: "Characteristics and Themes."
2. R. Laird Harris, "Leviticus," in *The Expositor's Bible Commentary*, vol. 2, ed. Frank E. Gaebelein (Grand Rapids, MI: Zondervan, 1990), 501–502.
3. Gordon J. Wenham, "The Book of Leviticus," in *The New International Commentary on the Old Testament*, vol. 3 (Grand Rapids, MI: Eerdmans, 1979), 16.
4. Wenham, 50.

LEVITICUS 1–7

Sacrifices Pleasing to God

These, then, are the regulations ... which the LORD gave Moses on Mount Sinai in the Desert of Sinai on the day he commanded the Israel-ites to bring their offerings to the LORD.
                                        LEVITICUS 7:37-38

1. For getting the most from Leviticus, one of the best guidelines is found in 2 Timothy 3:16-17, words that Paul wrote with the Old Testament first in view. He said that *all* Scripture is of great benefit to (a) teach us, (b) rebuke us, (c) correct us, and (d) train us in righteousness. Paul added that these Scriptures completely equip the person of God "for every good work." As you think seriously about those guidelines, in which of these areas do you especially want to experience the usefulness of Leviticus? Express your desire in a written prayer to God.

   _____

   _____

   _____

   _____

2. In Jeremiah 23:29, God says that His Word is like fire and like a hammer. He can use the Scriptures to burn away unclean thoughts and

13

For Thought and Discussion: As you launch into a closer look at Leviticus, how would you summarize what you already know about this book? And how would you describe the general impression that most Christians have of Leviticus?

For Further Study: In Exodus 40:34-38, notice the facts and imagery given in that book's concluding paragraph. How might this serve to prepare readers for what is coming in Leviticus?

desires in our hearts. He can also use Scripture, with hammer-like hardness, to crush and crumble our spiritual hardness. From your study of Leviticus, how do you most want to see the "fire-and-hammer" power of God's Word at work in your life? Express this longing in a written prayer to God.

_____

_____

_____

_____

_____

3. Think about these challenging words of Paul to his younger helper Timothy: "Do your best to present yourself to God as one approved, a worker who does not need to be ashamed and who correctly handles the word of truth" (2 Timothy 2:15). As you study God's word of truth in Leviticus, He calls you to be a "worker." It takes *work*—concentration and perseverance—to fully appropriate God's blessings for us in this book. Express here your commitment before God to work diligently in this study of Leviticus.

_____

_____

_____

_____

4. The book of Leviticus is linked strongly with Exodus, the book it follows. What are the most important themes and events, as you understand them, in the book of Exodus?

_____

_____

_____

_____

14

The LORD called (1:1). In Hebrew tradition, the opening verb "He called" also served as the title for this book. Leviticus continues God's gracious communication to His people.

---

5. Glance ahead through the pages of Leviticus, and look for a recurring principle or concept in each of the following verses: 11:44-45; 19:2; 20:26; 21:8. What is that principle or concept? Why is it important to God, and why is it important for you and for all of God's people in all ages?

_____

_____

_____

_____

_____

In Leviticus, God is in the details.

"Precisely because the rituals of Leviticus are so central to Old Testament thinking, they are often obscure to us, because the writers did not need to explain them to their contemporaries. Every Israelite knew why a particular sacrifice was offered on a specific occasion and what a certain gesture meant. For ourselves, every hint in the text must be grasped to understand these things, and a judicious reading between the lines is sometimes required."[1]

6. The first three chapters of Leviticus deal with the three most common types of offerings in

For Further Study:
The theme of holiness in Leviticus has its foundation in the two earlier books of the Pentateuch. How is God's holiness portrayed in Exodus 3:5 and 15:11? And how is holiness for God's people taught in these passages: Genesis 2:3; Exodus 12:16; 16:23; 20:8-11?

15

Israel. As you read over these chapters, imagine you are living in the time of Moses. Which details in these chapters would be of most interest to you?

_____

_____

_____

_____

7. In chapter 1, what exactly was a person to offer for a burnt offering, and what exactly was he to do with it? (See verses 2, 3, 5, 10, and 14.)

good income - large bull animal

small mium - small animal

(pigion or dove)

Blood dashed against the

sides of the altar

Brings an offering to the Lord (1:2). This phrase represents the central human action presented in these chapters. In Leviticus, God takes the initiative to direct His people in exactly how to come into His presence. It must be according to *His* instructions, not according to our own ideas.

Lay your hand on the head of the burnt offering (1:4). This symbolizes an acknowledgment that the animal serves as a substitute for the person bringing the offering.

8. From chapter 1 (as well as from 6:8-13), how would you summarize the most significant procedures to be followed by the priests in regard to burnt offerings?

Hand offering w/ bread, chees

turning.

_____

_____

16

9. In 1:4, what is given as the *purpose* for the burnt offering, and what is the significance of this? What does it teach us?

cleansing of impurities +
reconciled w/ God
God's holiness is satisfied

10. In chapter 2, what exactly was a person to offer for a grain offering, and what exactly was he to do with it? (See verses 1, 4-7, 11, and 13-15.)

first fruits of the field
lay hand on head of burnt offering
slaughter Bull before the Lord / before
Lord on alter, skin it and put parts on wood

11. From chapter 2 (as well as from 6:14-23), summarize the most significant procedures to be followed by the priests in regard to grain offerings.

flour + oil w/ incense + burn it

12. In chapter 3, what exactly was a person to offer for a fellowship offering (also called peace offering), and what exactly was he to do with it? (See verses 1, 6-7, and 12; look also at 7:12-13.)

a perfect animal from the herd, lay your
hand on its head, slaughter it, splash blood
on the altar + inner parts to burn on altar

"Using a little imagination every reader of the Old Testament soon realizes that these ancient sacrifices were very moving occasions. They make modern church services seem tame and dull by comparison. The ancient worshiper did

For Further Study:
The phrase "an aroma pleasing to the Lord" is found seventeen times in Leviticus. Earlier, its first use in Scripture was in Genesis 8:21, for an offering made by Noah after the Flood. Later, in the New Testament, how does Paul use this image in Ephesians 5:2 and Philippians 4:18?

For Further Study:
From Genesis 8:21-22; 2 Samuel 24:25; 2 Chronicles 29:7-8; and Job 1:5, what do we learn about the purpose burnt offerings accomplish?

For Further Study:
Hundreds of years
before the sacrifi-
cial regulations in
Leviticus were given
to Israel at Mount
Sinai, men were offer-
ing sacrifices to the
true God. Look at the
following passages
to see some of them:
Genesis 8:20; 22:13;
31:54; 46:1.

not just listen to the minister and sing a
few hymns. He was actively involved in
the worship."[2]

13. From chapter 3 (as well as from 7:11-34), what
were the most significant regulations to be followed in making fellowship (peace) offerings?

the type of animal + eyelash
blood on the altar.
peace offering - a shared meal

14. In chapters 4–6, we read about the sin offering and the guilt offering (also called trespass
offering). Summarize the kinds of offenses for
which these offerings were needed, according to
4:2,13,22,27; 5:1-4,15,17; and 6:2-3.

cleansing sin + defiled conditions
contamination, corruption,
for

The Lord said to Moses (4:1). More literally, "The
Lord spoke to Moses, saying . . ." Notice the
majestic repetition of this phrase at the beginning of chapters 6, 8, 11–25, and 27, and also at
5:14; 6:8,19,24; 7:22,28; 14:33; 21:16, 22:17,26;
23:9,23,26,33; 24:13. Take note of the natural
divisions they mark in the text.

"At the beginning of nearly every chapter,
and often several times within a chapter,
it says, 'The Lord spoke to Moses.' In other
words, all the laws are set within a narrative
framework. According to the author they
were revealed to Moses during Israel's
wilderness wanderings to meet specific
problems that arose at that time."[3]

15. For the sin offering and guilt offering, what exactly was the offending person to offer, and what was he to do with it? (See 4:1–6:7.)

a young bull without defect
lay hand on head, slaughter it, priest dipping in blood + sprinkle it 7 times in front of the curtain + put some on horns of altar + ... of altar

16. What were the most significant regulations to be followed in making sin and guilt offerings? (See 4:1–6:7, 6:24-30, and 7:1-10.)

17. What is stated as the *purpose* for the sin and guilt offerings (see 4:20,26,31,35; 5:6,10,13,16,18; 6:7), and what is the significance of this?

forgiveness for the community + individual – atonement for their sins

---

In this way the priest will make atonement for them before the Lord, *and they will be forgiven* (6:7). "To make atonement for sin is to have the penalty paid and the guilt removed. Here lies the significance and the glory of the Old Testament sacrifices, although they were not in themselves efficacious. They were only types and shadows (Hebrews 8:5) and therefore were repeated regularly and often, until the Great High Priest should come who would in a new priesthood offer a final sacrifice to effect atonement for his people."[4]

These are the regulations (6:9). Or, in many other English translations, "This is the law . . ." We see this phrase used repeatedly throughout

For Thought and Discussion: How serious is God about our holiness and the purity of our worship before Him? What are His expectations in this regard?

For Further Study: For the perpetual burnt offering mentioned in 6:8-9,12-13, compare Exodus 29:38-42. What did God want His people to experience and understand through this continuous offering?

Leviticus. These regulations are a part of God's continual grace toward His people.

> "The law was given in a context of grace. . . . God gave his law to Israel after they had been redeemed from Egypt, not as a means for securing their redemption. God's call to Israel to be his holy people preceded the revelation of the law at Sinai, but only obedience could make holiness a living reality."[5]

18. What do the provisions for the sin and guilt offerings teach us about God's holiness?

   Closeness to God
   purification

acceptance by God
forgivness !!
for admission into
His presence
desecration of
His Holy Name

19. Read closely the summary of these first seven chapters as stated in 7:37-38. What is the significance of each part of this summary statement?

   An offering to God
   sacrifice to God
   purification

> "In one sense . . . the whole ceremonial law in Leviticus is obsolete for the Christian. We are interested in the sacrifice of Christ, not in animal sacrifice. But in another sense the Levitical rituals are still of immense relevance. It was in terms of these sacrifices that Jesus himself and the early church understood his atoning

20

death. Leviticus provided the theological models for their understanding. If we wish to walk in our Lord's steps and think his thoughts after him, we must attempt to understand the sacrificial system of Leviticus. It was established by the same God who sent his Son to die for us; and in rediscovering the principles of Old Testament worship written there, we may learn something of the way we should approach a holy God."[6]

Optional Application: In order to better please God in our personal and corporate worship, what can we learn from Leviticus 1–7?

20. In what ways do you see God's *grace* in the system of sacrifices outlined here in Leviticus?

His willingness to forgive
His desire for a close +
personal relationship
His love for His people

21. What would you select as the key verse or passage in Leviticus 1–7 — the passage that best captures or reflects the dynamics of what these chapters are all about?

22. What would have been the special significance of these chapters for Israel as they faced their journey across the wilderness and a new national existence in the Promised Land?

to keep their faith and
to trust, to stay close
to God

21

23. List any lingering questions you have about Leviticus 1–7.

_____

_____

_____

For the Group

(In your first meeting, it may be helpful to turn to the front of this book and review together the section called "How to Use This Guide" on page 5.)

You may want to focus your discussion for lesson 1 especially on the following issues, themes, and concepts. (These things will likely reflect what group members have learned in their individual study of this week's passage, though they'll also have made discoveries in other areas as well.)

- The theological meaning of sacrifice, and the need for sacrifice
- How to please God
- The cost and injury of sin
- Atonement for sin and forgiveness of sin
- The meaning of peace
- Requirements for fellowship with God
- Appropriate worship of God

The following numbered questions in lesson 1 may stimulate your best and most helpful discussion: 6, 9, 17, 20, 21, 22, and 23.

Look also at the questions in the margin under the heading "For Thought and Discussion."

1. *New Geneva Study Bible* (Nashville: Thomas Nelson, 1995), introduction to Leviticus: "Characteristics and Themes."
2. Gordon J. Wenham, "The Book of Leviticus," in *The New International Commentary on the Old Testament,* vol. 3 (Grand Rapids, MI: Eerdmans, 1979), 55.
3. Wenham, 5.
4. R. Laird Harris, "Leviticus," in *The Expositor's Bible Commentary,* vol. 2, ed. Frank E. Gaebelein (Grand Rapids, MI: Zondervan, 1990), 523.
5. Wenham, 31.
6. Wenham, 36–37.

LEVITICUS 8–10

A Holy Priesthood

*This is what the Lord has commanded you to
do, so that the glory of the Lord may appear to
you.*

LEVITICUS 9:6

1. If you lived in the time of Moses and were one of
the priests serving at the altar of the tabernacle,
which details in these three chapters would be
of most interest to you?

   *anointing oil when someone
   comes to your house*

2. In chapter 8, what do you see as the most
important details in the procedure for conse-
crating Aaron and his sons to the priesthood?

   *purify yourself before
   offering on alter*

**For Thought and
Discussion:** Why
does God make provi-
sion for the establish-
ment of such leaders
among His people
as priests (in the Old
Testament) and pas-
tors and elders (in
the New Testament)?
What does this say
about the needs of
His people? What
does it say about
God's personal rela-
tionship with His
people?

Anointing oil (8:10). See the instructions for this
oil in Exodus 30:22-33.

For Further Study:
Compare the description in chapter 8 of the consecration of the priests with the instructions for this given in Exodus 29. What are the major parallels between the two passages?

"It is generally agreed that the anointing oil typifies the Holy Spirit. When kings were anointed, the Holy Spirit came on them (1 Samuel 10:1-6; 16:13). The word 'messiah' comes from the Hebrew word for 'anoint,' and the work of Christ began with such an anointing of the Holy Spirit. . . . Oil was widely used in lamps. As the lamp burned, the oil seemed to vanish into the air. Such a connection of oil and air possibly may have made the typology natural in the Hebrew culture. The Hebrew word *rûah* means either 'spirit' or 'wind, air, breath.' The seven-branched lampstand, perpetually fed with oil, is called a symbol of the Spirit in the Old Testament (Zechariah 4:2-6)."[1]

He poured some of the anointing oil on Aaron's head (8:12). See this image as David uses it poetically in Psalm 133:1-2.

The lobe of Aaron's right ear . . . the thumb of his right hand . . . the big toe of his right foot (8:23). The right ear symbolizes attentive obedience; the right thumb and toe symbolize man's initiative and action.

3. What are the most significant actions Moses takes in chapter 8?

Sprinkling of oil + blood

treated as priests

"Moses first acted as priest to consecrate the tabernacle, the altar, and Aaron and his sons. It is hard to overemphasize the work of Moses, the man of God. As the greatest of the Old Testament prophets, he was a type of Christ to come (Deuteronomy 18:15-19; John 7:40). As the first priest who instituted Israel's worship, Moses is a type of Christ the Great High Priest. Moses, the great lawgiver, received God's revelations face to face and was faithful in all God's house (Numbers 12:7-8). Yet even he was but a type and a shadow, far inferior to Christ the High Priest and Son over the house (Hebrews 3:1-6)."[2]

4. Notice how often the word *commanded* is used in chapter 8, and notice the repeated phrases in which this word is used. What does this teach us about God's view of the priesthood and about Moses' response to the Lord's instructions?

   same to do it my way

5. How closely does 8:18-21 conform with the regulations for burnt offerings given in Leviticus 1?

   hand on head, slaughter bull *same* *splash blood sides of altar, cut + burn skin, head + fat + burn wash internal organs + burn*

6. From chapter 9, summarize the most important actions taken by Moses and Aaron.

Aaron makes offerings for himself — then for the people when — Blessing the people after the sacrifices

7. What promise does Moses make to the people in 9:4 and 9:6, and what is its significance?

9:4 fellowship offering TODAY Lord
They will appear to you. 9:6 grain offering
of the Lord will appear to you.

8. What specific importance do you see in the word *atonement* as used twice in 9:7 and as signified in the actions of 9:8-21?

The Lord commanded it.
Burnt offerings - making atonement.

9. Reflect on the moment of great worship, joy, fear, and reverence described in 9:23-24. If you had been there in that moment, what might you have remembered most about it in later years?

glory of Lord in fire.

"The cloud of the divine glory is luminescent, enveloping the fire into which it turns at night. Here, the emergence of the fire is a dramatic sign of God's self-revelation and of divine favor in accepting the sacrifice."[3]

26

10. If you were in Aaron's shoes, what do you think these events in chapter 9 would mean most to you? What thoughts and emotions would you most likely experience at the time? In later years, what would you cherish most about this day?

purify yourself first to make an offering.

2 assuring people of cleansing + forgiveness

didn't offer guilt offering

report to that person first than to the Lord

Aaron lifted his hands toward the people and blessed them (9:22). Many Bible teachers have speculated that the words Aaron spoke here were those of the beautiful blessing recorded later in Numbers 6:24-26.

---

11. The events in chapter 9 reflect the first service in the tabernacle following the dedication of Aaron and his sons to the priesthood. What important principles and precedents are being established here?

purification + peace offerings · acknowledge sin + need for forgiveness cleansing + atonement

young purification, meat offering, & peace for the people

to be accepted by God priests had to first cleanse themselves.

12. From chapter 10, explain the offense committed by Nadab and Abihu and your understanding of why it was wrong.

1) they offered fire + incense before the Lord. They were being anointed w/oil + had not done the current offerings

from their own container not from the altar.

Fire came out from the presence of the LORD (10:2). This same phrase is found just a few verses earlier, in 9:24, when the Lord accepted Aaron's offering.

13. What do the Lord's words in 10:3 indicate about His character and His intentions? Express this in your own words, and elaborate on its meaning.

Do only as you are commanded

He wants to bless

his people.

Distinguish between the holy and the common (10:10). See also 11:47 and 20:25. The Hebrew for "distinguish" or "make a distinction" in these verses has the root connotation of "to separate" or "to divide." It's also found in the Creation account, where we read that God "separated the light from the darkness" (Genesis 1:4).

---

14. How would you explain the meaning of the Lord's words in 10:10?

priests are separate from

the people

15. What significance do you see in the incident described in 10:16-20, especially as it relates to what has happened earlier in chapter 10?

Moses thought they disobeyed

The Lord by not eating the sin

offering but they probably could

not eat after seeing sons die

16. Summarize the significant lessons God wanted His people to learn from all that happened in Leviticus 10.

to obey + be faithful —
all the people are sinful
+ need offerings from the
priests
don't doubt Gods command

"Whoever scorns instruction will pay for it, but whoever respects a command is rewarded." (Proverbs 13:13)

17. In the chapters of Leviticus that we've studied so far (1–10), what sense do you get of the importance of our right worship toward God?

He is holy — these
people are his chosen
ones.

"Leviticus is a continuation of Exodus. Exodus ends with the setting up of the tabernacle. Leviticus proceeds with the directions for the offerings. Then Leviticus tells how the priests began their ministry using the terms of the directions already given in Exodus."[4]

18. In what ways do you see God's *grace* for His people in the kind of priesthood initiated here in Leviticus?

The only way to T for n the people to
gain access to the Lord was
thru the priests

Optional Application: God has declared to His people, "You will be for me a *kingdom of priests*" (Exodus 19:6, emphasis added) and "You are a chosen people, *a royal priesthood*" (1 Peter 2:9, emphasis added). How does what you're learning in Leviticus add to the meaning of this calling that all believers have from God? And what does this calling mean personally for you?

For Further Study: Contrast the Old Testament priesthood with the priesthood of Jesus as described in Hebrews 7:23–8:6.

29

_____

_____

19. What would you select as the key verse or passage in Leviticus 8–10 — the passage that best captures or reflects the dynamics of what these chapters are all about?

_____

_____

_____

20. What would have been the special significance of these chapters for Israel as they faced their journey across the wilderness and a new national existence in the Promised Land?

Keep the commandments

Keep the offerings

Keep faithful

21. List any lingering questions you have about Leviticus 8–10.

_____

_____

_____

_____

For the Group

You may want to focus your discussion for lesson 2 especially on the following issues, themes, and concepts. (These will likely reflect what group members have learned in their individual study of this week's passage, though they'll also have made discoveries in other areas as well.)

- The meaning of consecration for service to God
- The requirements for serving God
- Appropriate worship of God
- The danger of going against God's ways and laws

The following numbered questions in lesson 2 may stimulate your best and most helpful discussion: 1, 9, 10, 16, 17, 18, 19, 20, and 21.

Look also at the questions in the margin under the heading "For Thought and Discussion."

1. R. Laird Harris, "Leviticus," in *The Expositor's Bible Commentary,* vol. 2, ed. Frank E. Gaebelein (Grand Rapids, MI: Zondervan, 1990), 561.
2. Harris, 559.
3. Robert Alter, *The Five Books of Moses* (New York: Norton, 2004), 578.
4. Harris, 559.

LEVITICUS 11–15

Clean and Unclean

I am the LORD your God; consecrate yourselves and be holy, because I am holy.

LEVITICUS 11:44

1. In these chapters, how do you see God's concern for His people's physical health and well-being?

_____

_____

_____

_____

For Thought and Discussion: As you understand it, what is the theological and biblical meaning of the terms *holy* and *clean*? What distinction, if any, is there between them?

"Holy" and "Clean" — A Profound Emphasis in Leviticus

"'Holy' (Hebrew *qādôsh*) and its cognate terms, e.g., 'sanctify,' 'holiness,' occur 152 times in Leviticus (about 20 percent of the total occurrences in the Old Testament). "Unclean" (*tāmē'*) and its cognates occur 132 times (more than 50 percent of the total Old Testament occurrences). "Clean" (*tāhôr*) and related terms occur 74 times (35 percent of the total). "Profane" (*hillēl*) occurs 14 times in Leviticus out of 66 references in the OT."[1]

(continued on page 34)

For Further Study:
Compare Leviticus 11 with the passage on clean and unclean foods in Deuteronomy 14:6-19. What are the most significant parallels?

(continued from page 33)

"The notion underlying holiness and cleanness was wholeness and normality. The priests, for example, had to be free from physical deformity (21:5-6, 17ff.). Mixed crops, mixed clothing, and mixed marriages are incompatible with holiness (18:23; 19:19).

"The same insistence on wholeness underlies the uncleanness laws in this chapter [11]. The animal world is divided into three spheres: those that fly in the air, those that walk on the land, and those that swim in the seas (cf. Gen. 1:20-30). Each sphere has a particular mode of motion associated with it. Birds have two wings with which to fly, and two feet for walking; fish have fins and scales with which to swim; land animals have hoofs to run with. The clean animals are those that conform to these standard pure types. Those creatures which in some way transgress the boundaries are unclean. . . .

"There is a parallel between the holiness looked for in man and the cleanness of animals: man must conform to the norms of moral and physical perfection, and animals must conform to the standards of the animal group to which they belong."[2]

"Granted that its root means separateness, the next idea that emerges is of the Holy as wholeness and completeness. Much of Leviticus is taken up with stating the physical perfection that is required of things presented in the temple and of persons approaching it."[3]

2. What underlying moral principles and values do you see behind the regulations in Leviticus 11 regarding clean and unclean animals?

_____

_____

_____

_____

_____

"The LORD is gracious and compassionate. . . . The LORD is good to all; he has compassion on all he has made." (Psalm 145:8-9) "Leviticus has to be read in line with Psalm 145:8-9: the God of Israel has compassion for all that he made. His love for his animal creation lies behind his laws against eating and touching their carcasses. The flocks and herds of the people of Israel are brought under the covenant that God made with their owners, and the other animals benefit from the promise he made in Genesis after the flood, that he would guarantee the regularity of the seasons and the fertility of the ground."[4]

"The Israelites are expected to set themselves apart from the natural world to which they belong just as they are required to set themselves apart from the nations with which, of necessity, they participate in political, economic, and cultural intercourse. Thus they are forbidden the flesh of whole classes of living creatures."[5]

"It is clear that classifying an animal as 'unclean' is not the same as declaring that animal 'evil': God cares for all beasts, clean and unclean alike."[6]

3. Look at what the apostle Peter was told about unclean food in Acts 10:9-16 (compare also Acts 11:4-17). How can this increase our understanding of Leviticus 11?

_____

_____

_____

For Further Study:
Review the New
Testament promise of
our *cleansing* through
Christ in 1 John 1:7,9,
as well as similar
statements of this
truth in 1 Corinthians
6:11, Ephesians
5:26, and Titus 2:14.
How does this New
Testament truth
relate to the kind
of cleansing taught
throughout Leviticus
11–15?

**Optional
Application:** Take
time to worship God
for His holiness. What
can you express to
Him about the deep
and profound mean-
ing of His holiness to
you?

4. Notice the various regulations about animal
carcasses mentioned throughout the passage in
11:24-40. What do these imply about God's view
of life and death?

_____

_____

_____

_____

I am the LORD, who brought you up out of Egypt
(11:45). "In Leviticus, whenever the exodus
from Egypt is mentioned it is always as a
motive for keeping the law."[7] See also 18:3 and
23:43.

---

5. Review carefully the statements God makes in
11:44-45 about Himself—and about us. Look
ahead to see how these thoughts are repeated in
19:2 and 20:7 and 26. State as fully as you can,
in your own words, what God wants His people
to understand in these statements.

_____

_____

_____

_____

"Holiness characterizes God himself and
all that belongs to him. . . . Holiness is
intrinsic to God's character."[8]

6. Relate the teaching in Leviticus 11:44-45 to
the words of Jesus in Matthew 5:48, as well as
to the following New Testament passages on
holiness: 2 Corinthians 7:1, Hebrews 12:14, and
1 Peter 1:15-16. How would you summarize
biblical teaching on the holiness that Christians
should pursue?

_____

_____

_____

_____

7. Summarize the regulations given in Leviticus 12 for purification after childbirth.

_____

_____

_____

"A woman who has just given birth is considered unclean. The loss of blood signifies that one is incomplete and unclean."[9]

8. Summarize the procedures presented in Leviticus 13:1-46 for identifying and dealing with disease.

_____

_____

_____

"These laws on skin diseases are again eloquent testimony to the importance of purity and holiness in ancient Israel. Anyone might fall victim to these complaints and face the prospect of being cut off from his family and friends for the rest of his days. Yet it was considered so important to preserve the purity of the tabernacle and the holiness of the nation that individuals and families might be forced to suffer a good deal.

Optional Application: How does your personal pursuit of holiness line up with what the Scriptures teach about this? In what areas of life does God want you to rely more on His Holy Spirit to strengthen your experience of holiness? Ask God to help you in this.

For Further Study: According to what you see in Luke 2:22-24, how did Mary and Joseph apply these laws from Leviticus 12 at the time Jesus was born?

For Further Study:
Keep in mind the
statements in
Leviticus about
God's holiness — and
the need for His
people to be clean
and holy — as you
take a fresh look at
the prophet Isaiah's
experience in Isaiah
6:1-7. How does this
passage reinforce and
amplify what you're
learning in Leviticus?

Individual discomfort was not allowed
to jeopardize the spiritual welfare of the
nation, for God's abiding presence with
his people depended on uncleanness
being excluded from their midst."[10]

"The fact of the matter is that the
ancients perceived and described diseases and their symptoms differently
than does modern Western medicine,
and some conditions that they under-
stood to be a single malady may actually have been a variety of diseases, not
all of them intrinsically related. Scholarly
attempts to equate the various conditions reported here with specific der-
matological disorders have had only limited success. A certain lack of specificity
in the translation of the quasi-medical
language of this section seems prudent
and, indeed, appropriate."[11]

"Modern readers should not confuse
this kind of 'uncleanness' [in Leviticus
13:3] with 'under God's condemnation,'
nor even with 'excluded from the love
of the community': the purpose of this
law is to prevent what is unclean from
coming into contact with what is holy
(a contact that would be dangerous for
the unclean person and for the whole
community)."[12]

9. Leviticus 13:47-49 identifies a "disease" in cloth
   or leather, which would most likely be mold.
   (The Hebrew term often translated as "mildew"
   in 13:47-49 is the same word translated as
   "leprosy" or "disease" throughout the earlier

part of chapter 13.) Summarize the procedures for identifying and dealing with this.

_____

_____

_____

_____

"The modern mind sees little in common between human skin disease and mold affecting garments or other household articles. The ancient Israelites saw things differently. They used the same word for both, _tsāra'at_. . . . From the standpoint of appearance, there are areas of resemblance between the two complaints. Both are abnormal surface conditions that disfigure the outside of the skin or garment. Both cause the surface to flake or peel."[13]

10. In the regulations given to the people of Israel in chapter 13, what underlying moral principles and values do you see behind them, and how might they have relevance for believers today?

_____

_____

_____

_____

11. Summarize the procedures prescribed in 14:1-32 for cleansing from skin disease.

_____

_____

_____

Hyssop (14:4). This aromatic plant was used often in ceremonial purification. See Exodus 12:22 (in the original Passover instructions), as well as Numbers 19:18 and Psalm 51:7.

He is to release the live bird (14:7). This is like what will be done with the live scapegoat in 16:6-10.

12. Summarize the procedures prescribed in 14:33-53 for cleaning houses.

_____

_____

_____

When you enter the land of Canaan (14:34). This verse seems to indicate that at the time of the events in Leviticus, Moses and the people expected to enter the Promised Land relatively soon. (See also 23:10 and 25:2.) Later, the tragic events recorded in Numbers 13–14 would lead to a forty-year wilderness sojourn for the nation.

13. Throughout chapters 14–15, how is water used as a cleansing agent?

_____

_____

_____

14. In regard to the regulations given to the people of Israel in chapter 15, what underlying moral principles and values do you see behind them, and how might they have relevance for believers today?

_____

_____

_____

"The more closely the text is studied, the more closely Leviticus reveals itself as a modern religion, legislating for justice between persons and persons, between God and his people, and between people and animals."[14]

"All these regulations are reflections of a pervasive spiritual seriousness grounded in a comprehensive, coherent conception of reality."[15]

15. Taken together, what impression do chapters 11–15 give you of what "cleanness" and "uncleanness" mean in God's sight and why this distinction is important?

_____

_____

_____

_____

16. What is implied or assumed in chapters 11–15 about God's rightful authority to determine the proper use for *everything* He has created? And why is this important for His people to grasp?

_____

_____

_____

_____

17. In what ways do you see God's *grace* in the regulations given in this part of Leviticus?

_____

_____

_____

_____

18. What would you select as the key verse or passage in Leviticus 11–15—the passage that best captures or reflects the dynamics of what these chapters are all about?

_____

_____

_____

19. What would have been the special significance of these chapters for Israel as they faced their journey across the wilderness and a new national existence in the Promised Land?

_____

_____

_____

20. List any lingering questions you have about Leviticus 11–15.

_____

_____

_____

For the Group

You may want to focus your discussion for lesson 3 especially on the following issues, themes, and concepts. (These will likely reflect what group members have learned in their individual study of this week's passage, though they'll also have made discoveries in other areas as well.)

- Being holy and clean in God's sight
- Completeness and wholeness in God's sight

The following numbered questions in lesson 3 may stimulate your best and most helpful discussion: 1, 5, 6, 14, 15, 17, 18, 19, and 20.

Remember to look also at the "For Thought and Discussion" questions in the margin.

1. Gordon J. Wenham, "The Book of Leviticus," in *The New International Commentary on the Old Testament,* vol. 3 (Grand Rapids, MI: Eerdmans, 1979), 5. "Statistics are from *Theologisches Handworterbuch zum AT,* I, 571, 647, 665; II, 593."
2. Wenham, 169–170.
3. Mary Douglas, *Purity and Danger* (London: Routledge & Kegan Paul, 1966), 63.
4. Mary Douglas, *Leviticus as Literature* (New York: Oxford University Press, 1999), 1–2.
5. Robert Alter, *The Five Books of Moses* (New York: Norton, 2004), 585.
6. *ESV Study Bible* (Wheaton, IL: Crossway, 2008), at Leviticus 11:1-47.
7. Wenham, 31.
8. Wenham, 22.
9. *ESV Study Bible*, at Leviticus 12:1-8.
10. Wenham, 203.
11. Alter, 591.
12. *ESV Study Bible*, at Leviticus 13:3.
13. Wenham, 201.
14. Mary Douglas, *Leviticus as Literature*, 2.
15. Alter, 545.

LEVITICUS 16

Atonement

This is to be a lasting ordinance for you: Atonement is to be made once a year for all the sins of the Israelites.

LEVITICUS 16:34

1. Proverbs 2:1-5 tells about the sincere person who truly longs for wisdom and understanding and searches the Scriptures for it as if treasure were buried there. Such a person, this passage says, will come to understand the fear of the Lord and discover the knowledge of God. As you continue exploring Leviticus, what "buried treasure" would you like God to help you find here—to show you what God and His wisdom are really like? If you have this desire, how would you express it in a prayer to God?

_____

_____

_____

_____

2. Chapter 16 has been called the key to the book of Leviticus. Why might this be so?

_____

_____

_____

For Thought and Discussion: What does the word *atonement* mean to you, both in everyday language and as a theological term? How exactly does atonement accomplish forgiveness?

"The Day of Atonement, when annual atonement was made for the sins of the nation, was the holiest day in the Old Testament calendar. It fell in the Hebrew seventh month (October) and involved the offering of various sacrifices, the entry of the high priest into the Most Holy Place . . . and the dispatch of a goat into the wilderness carrying the people's sins."[1]

3. What is significant about the mention of Aaron's sons in verse 1?

   The Lord spoke to Moses AFTER the death of Aarons 2 sons.

4. What does verse 2 indicate to us about God's holiness?

   Only you obey God only go into the holy place for atonement of sins

5. What repeated emphasis do you find in verses 11, 17, and 24?

   makes atonement for his own sins & his household

6. What happens in Leviticus 16:1-10 as part of the Day of Atonement, and what is the significance and symbolism of each of these actions?

   sin offerings - he makes sins burnt offering for himself first, then (bull)

46

handwritten at top: God forgiving me

handwritten: for the people (goats) one for offering one for scapegoat removing the guilt

He is to take the two goats and present them before the Lord (16:7). "Two goats were taken to bear the people's sins. One was killed as a sin offering; the other was sent off into the desert to bear away the propitiation for sins by death and complete removal of the sins for which atonement was made. Many a person today who suffers from what is called a guilt complex could profit by a study of this ritual for the atonement and removal of sin."[2]

Optional Application: Reflecting on the fragrant incense offering of Leviticus 16:12-13, notice how Jesus and His death are described in Ephesians 5:1-2. With this image in mind, what are we told to do in response? In sincere prayer, ask God to help you respond this way.

7. What happens in 16:11-14 as part of the Day of Atonement, and what is the significance and symbolism of each of these actions?

handwritten: kill for sin offering for himself & family Burn incense on the altar so he will not die. Sprinkle bull blood on atonement cover 7 times. Smoke shielded him from the Lord

Fragrant incense (16:12). See Exodus 30:34-38, which gives regulations for how this incense is blended and used.

The tablets of the covenant law (16:13). The Ten Commandments. See Exodus 31:18.

8. What happens in 16:15-19 as part of the Day of Atonement, and what is the significance and symbolism of each of these actions?

handwritten: he does the same thing for the people - for their forgiveness of sin because of their uncleanliness + rebellion. Aaron goes in alone.

47

For Further Study: In the New Testament, how is the purification role of blood explained in Hebrews 9:19-22?

then Aaron removes his holy linen garments & put on reg. garments (priest) then sacrifice burnt offering for himself & for the people, to make atonement for both.

9. What happens in 16:20-28 as part of the Day of Atonement, and what is the significance and symbolism of each of these actions?

Aaron lay both hands on head of goat & confess all the wickedness & rebellion of the Israelites, then releases the goat to the desert.

10. What special significance do you see in the phrase "all their sins" in verse 21?

their wickedness & rebellion - (sins) what will be left done & undone

11. In the New Testament, to teach us about the sacrifice of Christ, Hebrews 9 often refers back to the Day of Atonement. Summarize each of these passages and explain how it builds on the meaning of the Day of Atonement as taught in Leviticus 16:

Hebrews 9:1-10

The Tabernacle was set up the same & used the same by the Jews

Hebrews 9:11-14

their cleaning for prevness was outwardly cleansing Jesus blood is whole cleansing

Hebrews 9:15-22

Jesus death set us free effect can only take place thru blood

Hebrews 9:23-28

For Further Study:
How do Psalm 103:12 and Micah 7:19 reflect the meaning behind the second goat on the Day of Atonement — the goat that was sent away?

priests had to go every year to make the sacrifice.

Jesus died once for all forgiveness of sin

12. Take a look also at Hebrews 13:11-13, Romans 3:21-26 and 6:5, and 1 Peter 2:24. How do these passages bring to mind the Day of Atonement and with what significance?

Heb 13:11 to be outside the camp is to be unclean. Jesus suffered outside the Jerusalem gates.
Romans we are justified by His grace 6:5 be united thru His resurrection 1Peter 2:24 Jesus bore our sins on a tree

13. From Leviticus 16:29-34, summarize what God wanted His people to *do* in regard to the Day of Atonement?

rest — do not work
deny yourself of everything (even eating)

14. Also from Leviticus 16:29-34, summarize what God wanted His people to *understand* in regard to the Day of Atonement.

1) it would be done every year - a lasting ordinance 10th day of 7th month
2) you will be cleansed of your sins

Optional Application: With the imagery of the Day of Atonement in mind, review the truth of our purification in Christ as proclaimed in Hebrews 9:13-14. Give thanks to the Lord for the grace He thereby offers us. How does a better understanding of Leviticus 16 enrich our appreciation of the gracious truth stated in Hebrews 9:13-14?

Deny yourselves (16:29,31). This is generally thought to refer to fasting. The Day of Atonement was thus the only regularly appointed day of fasting for Israel. See also Psalm 35:13 and Isaiah 58:3.

15. In Leviticus 16:16 and 16:34, what is the stated reason for the Day of Atonement?

    Cleanse from sins

16. Also notice in Leviticus 16:34 the required frequency for the Day of Atonement. Why do you think God chose this particular frequency, rather than more often or less often?

The Scarlet Thread *Jesus blood*

"The historic view of the Old Testament sacrificial system is that the death of the sacrificial victim is the God-given type of the death of Christ and that Christ by his death paid the penalty for our sins. The sacrifices were substitutionary in type and symbol. Life was for life, and the one who trusted in God's substitute for sin was freed from penalty. This is most clearly expressed in the Book of Hebrews. It says in sum: 'By one sacrifice he [Christ] has made perfect forever those who are being made holy' (10:14); 'we have confidence to enter the Most Holy Place by the blood of Jesus, by a new and living way opened for us through the curtain, that is, his body' (10:19-20).

"Romans is equally explicit: 'God presented him [Christ] as a sacrifice of atonement, through faith in his blood. He did this to demonstrate his justice . . . so as to be just and the one who justifies those who have faith in Jesus' (3:25-26). It is of some interest that both of these classic passages are directly dependent on the ritual of the Day of Atonement as outlined in Leviticus.

"This doctrine of the typological blood of the sacrifices and the efficacious blood of Christ . . . has been called the scarlet line of redemption that begins in Abel's sacrifice in Genesis and climaxes in the blood of the Lamb slain from the creation of the world in Revelation (13:8). Jesus said it plainly, 'I lay down my life for the sheep' (John 10:15)."[3]

17. What are the most important ways in which you see God's *grace* in how He established the Day of Atonement for His people?

It was difficult for Him but he made it easy for us.

18. What would you select as the key verse in Leviticus 16 — the one that best captures or reflects the dynamics of what these chapters are all about?

19. What would have been the special significance of Leviticus 16 for Israel as they faced their journey across the wilderness and a new national existence in the Promised Land?

20. List any lingering questions you have about Leviticus 16.

_____

_____

_____

_____

For the Group

You may want to focus your discussion for lesson 4 especially on the following issues, themes, and concepts. (These will likely reflect what group members have learned in their individual study of this week's passage, though they'll also have made discoveries in other areas as well.)

- Atonement for sin and forgiveness for sin
- Propitiation for sin
- Requirements for fellowship with God
- The meaning of sacrifice for sin

The following numbered questions in lesson 4 may stimulate your best and most helpful discussion: 2, 11, 12, 13, 14, 17, 18, 19, and 20.

Remember to look also at the "For Thought and Discussion" questions in the margin.

1. *New Geneva Study Bible* (Nashville: Thomas Nelson, 1995), at Leviticus 16:1-34.
2. R. Laird Harris, "Leviticus," in *The Expositor's Bible Commentary*, vol. 2, ed. Frank E. Gaebelein (Grand Rapids, MI: Zondervan, 1990), 588.
3. Harris, 520.

LEVITICUS 17–22

A Call to Holiness

> *Do not profane my holy name, for I must be*
> *acknowledged as holy by the Israelites. I am the*
> *LORD, who made you holy and who brought you*
> *out of Egypt to be your God. I am the LORD.*
>   LEVITICUS 22:32-33

This section of Leviticus is sometimes known as the Holiness Code because of the standards it gives for God's people.

"The principles underlying the Old Testament are valid and authoritative for the Christian, but the particular applications found in the Old Testament may not be. The moral principles are the same today, but insofar as our situation often differs from the Old Testament setting, the application of the principles in our society may well be different too."[1]

1. Describe the regulations outlined for the place of sacrifice in 17:1-9, and record what you see as God's primary intention for these regulations.

only make sacrifices to
the Lord at the entrance to
the Tent of the meeting – Priest

For Thought and Discussion: To your best understanding, what does *life* really mean in its richest, God-intended dimensions?

Optional Application: Keeping in mind Leviticus 18:5 and God's promise there of life, take a moment to rejoice before the Lord in the new life He has given you in Christ. You may want to reflect on these Scriptures to increase your joy: Psalms 16:11; 36:9; John 6:63; 7:38; Romans 6:4; 8:11.

to sprinkle blood against altar follow God's laws because God is holy

2. Read carefully the section regarding the sanctity of blood in 17:10-16. Why is such importance placed here on blood?

blood is used to make atonement — the life of a being or animal is in its blood.

3. Reference is made in 17:11 to the connection between blood and atonement. How would you explain this connection in your own words?

blood is atonement — preparing us for Jesus's blood (for our sins)

4. Look carefully in 18:1-5 at what God's people are told *not* to do and what they're told positively to *do*. And notice especially the promise God makes in verse 5. What does this teach us about ourselves as human beings and about God's commands?

not to do as they did in Egypt or Canaan; do obey my laws + decrees. God is Lord

The Promise of Life

We can view God's promise of life in Leviticus 18:5 within the broader New Testament context of the gospel and its promise of salvation by grace through faith.

"Leviticus 18:5 promises a good life here and eternal life hereafter in the whole OT context of faith in God and trust in his promises, including those given in the symbolism and typology of the sacrifices detailed in this very Book of Leviticus.

54

"No, Leviticus 18:5 does not teach salvation by works. It teaches that the Old Testament believers who trusted God and obeyed him from the heart received life abundant both here and hereafter. . . .

"Regardless of various applications of Leviticus 18:5, it would seem that the things here required to be done include all the laws of God — including keeping the laws of morality and the rituals of atonement and worship in the tabernacle. Observance of these laws in an attitude of faith resulted in spiritual life and power for the godly Israelite. But, as Leviticus 19:17 and other verses show, the Lord required more than mere external obedience and ritual. The Lord desired a circumcised heart (Deuteronomy 30:6). Therefore it is best to take Leviticus 18:5 as a command to keep all God's laws by faith and thus attain a full spiritual life."[2]

"For the Old Testament writers life means primarily physical life. But it is clear that in this and similar passages more than mere existence is being promised. What is envisaged is a happy life in which a man enjoys God's bounty of health, children, friends, and prosperity. Keeping the law is the path to divine blessing, to a happy and fulfilled life in the present (Leviticus 26:3-13; Deuteronomy 28:1-14). . . . But it is Jesus and Paul who insist that the full meaning of life is eternal life. . . . In John's Gospel man must keep the new law — the word of Christ. 'Whoever obeys my word will never see death' (John 8:51)."[3]

For Further Study:
In Ezekiel 20, we find a unique summary of Israel's history that God gives through His prophet. Within this prophecy, the promise of life in Leviticus 18:5 is brought up three times — in verses 11, 13, and 21. See a similar reference to Leviticus 18:5 in Nehemiah 9:29. Notice as well what Jesus said in Luke 10:28. How does this further emphasis from God interpret and reinforce the meaning of the promise in Leviticus 18:5?

For Further Study:
Compare the promise of life in Leviticus 18:5 with the extended promise of life in Deuteronomy 30:15-20. What parts of the Deuteronomy passage are reflected, implied, or assumed in Leviticus 18:1-5?

5. In the New Testament, Paul used Leviticus 18:5 as a springboard into the gospel. Read how he did this in Romans 10:5-13 and Galatians 3:11-14. In your own words, how would you summarize the relationship of Leviticus 18:5 to the gospel of Jesus Christ?

by your faith, not laws, & your confession that Jesus is Lord, you are saved

"You must not do as they do" — this call in Leviticus 18:3 for nonconformity to the secular world is re-iterated in many New Testament passages. How do you see it expressed in Romans 12:2, 2 Corinthians 6:14-17, Ephesians 4:17-20, 1 Peter 1:14-15, and 1 John 2:15-17.

Optional Application: "You must not do as they do" (18:3). As you think especially of how nonconformity to the world is strongly emphasized in the New Testament (see above), what does this biblical directive require most from *you* in your life at this time?

"Paul in Galatians 3:12 (et al.) is referring to the Old Testament as the Judaizers misinterpreted it. This false interpretation of the law led to death. It could save no one but rather was a yoke of bondage. . . . Paul quoted Leviticus 18:5 as the Judaizers used it, but he answered the misinterpretation with abundant quotations of the Old Testament giving the true interpretation of the law. . . . Paul was saying, 'The Pharisees and the Judaizers teach that the law offers salvation by works, but that is a misuse of the law that cannot contradict the promise of grace.'"[4]

6. From chapter 18, describe the regulations outlined regarding unlawful sexual relations, and record what you see as God's primary intention for these regulations.

   obey my laws
   These are sins in
   God's eyes.

7. How would you summarize the right understanding and attitudes concerning human sexuality that are taught to God's people in chapter 18?

   God formed a new culture
   w/ them.

8. In the laws mentioned in chapter 19, how many of the Ten Commandments can you see referred to either directly or indirectly? (You can refer back to the list of the commandments in Exodus 20.)

Ex 19: 3,4, 11, 12, 13, 15, 16, 17, 18, 30

10

9. From 19:1-18, describe the regulations outlined regarding the people's behavior toward each other, and record what you see as God's primary intention for these regulations.

protection for the poor care for the poor, fellowship offering, leave part of your field harvest for the poor.

don't bear a grudge

forgiveness

Love your neighbor as yourself (19:18). Review how Jesus cites this passage in Mark 12:28-31.

10. Notice again how 19:2 and 20:7 and 26 repeat and reflect the holiness teaching that was given in 11:44-45. Now that you've studied additional chapters in Leviticus, what additions would you make to your answer for question 5 in lesson 3 about holiness?

11. In Leviticus 19:19-37, we see the application of this principle to various areas of life: "Holiness means more than mere separation, but it always signifies that something is set apart

For Thought and Discussion: Why do you think God is so opposed to the kind of sacrifice mentioned in 20:1-5?

in its proper sphere."[5] What are some ways in which you recognize this principle in the listed regulations? *The fruit will increase for 5 yrs*

The blood— human remains in a being that belongs to God

Love 'your neighbor as yourself.

clean unclean / separation

12. Summarize the regulations given in 20:1-21, and record what you see as God's primary intention for them.

1 Consecrate yourself & be holy, keep Gods laws / decrees + follow them +2 God was building a nation to make a positive influence on the world.

13. In Matthew 23:23, Jesus said the most important aspects of the law are "justice, mercy and faithfulness." How do you see these important aspects reflected in the laws presented in Leviticus, and especially chapter 20?

_____

_____

_____

_____

14. How would you summarize the exhortations toward holiness given in 20:22-26 and the reasoning behind them?

God didn't withhold good + set rules that would keep them faithful + holy.

15. What do we learn in 20:3 and 22:2 and 32 about God's name? How would you express in your own words what God wants His people to understand about this?

He wants you to honor His name + respect Him (not profane - treat w/ irreverance/disrespect) 2 He is holy + wants His people to be holy.

Optional Application: In what possible ways might you be most tempted to "profane" God's name (20:3; 22:2,32)? What does it mean for you to keep God's name holy, and what personal importance does this have?

Optional Application: In order to better please God in our personal and corporate worship, what can we learn from Leviticus 21–22?

16. Summarize the regulations for the priesthood and for worship given in chapters 21 and 22, and record what you see as God's primary intention for them.

priests must be "clean" God wanted the priests to serve Him + the people + help the people worship Him.

17. What in Leviticus 21 reflects most impressively the need for holiness among the priests?

the priests must be as close to God as they could the perfect *God first*

18. What in Leviticus 22 reflects most impressively the need for holiness in the people's offerings?

Because God is without blemish so must their offerings - to be holy

19. In what ways do you see God's *grace* in the commands and regulations given in this part of Leviticus?

_____

_____

_____

59

"New Testament theology makes full use of the idea of holiness. All Christians are holy, 'saints' in most English translations. That is, they have been called by God to be his people just as ancient Israel had been (Colossians 1:2; 1 Peter 1:2; 2:9-10; cf. Exodus 19:5-6). But this state of holiness must find expression in holy living (Colossians 1:22-23; 1 Peter 1:15). Sanctification is expressed through obedience to the standard of teaching (Romans 6:17-19), just as in Leviticus through obedience to the law. Peter urges his readers to make the motto of Leviticus their own: 'Be holy, because I am holy' (1 Peter 1:16). The imitation of God is a theme that unites the ethics of Old and New Testaments (cf. Matthew 5:48; 1 Corinthians 11:1)."[6]

20. What would you select as the key verse or passage in Leviticus 17–22 — the passage that best captures or reflects the dynamics of what these chapters are all about?

_____

_____

_____

21. What would have been the special significance of these chapters for Israel as they faced their journey across the wilderness and a new national existence in the Promised Land?

_____

_____

_____

22. In Psalm 119:45, the psalmist says to God, "I will walk about in freedom, for I have sought out your precepts." As you think about the many precepts and laws given in Leviticus, in what ways can you see them offering freedom to God's people? And how would disobeying these commands bring bondage?

1 we have freedom because of God's forgiveness. 2 disobeying brings sin & distruction

23. List any lingering questions you have about Leviticus 17–22.

For the Group

You may want to focus your discussion for lesson 5 especially on the following issues, themes, and concepts. (These will likely reflect what group members have learned in their individual study of this week's passage, though they'll also have made discoveries in other areas as well.)

- Holiness
- The meaning of life in its true fullness
- Our obligations to others
- The meaning of consecration for service to God
- The requirements for serving God
- Appropriate worship of God

The following numbered questions in lesson 5 may stimulate your best and most helpful discussion: 2, 3, 4, 5, 7, 13, 15, 19, 20, 21, 22, and 23.

Remember to look also at the "For Thought and Discussion" questions in the margin.

1. Gordon J. Wenham, "The Book of Leviticus," in *The New International Commentary on the Old Testament*, vol. 3 (Grand Rapids, MI: Eerdmans, 1979), 35.
2. R. Laird Harris, "Leviticus," in *The Expositor's Bible Commentary*, vol. 2, ed. Frank E. Gaebelein (Grand Rapids, MI: Zondervan, 1990), 598.
3. Wenham, 253.
4. Harris, 598.
5. *ESV Study Bible* (Wheaton, IL: Crossway, 2008), at Leviticus 19:19-37.
6. Wenham, 25.

LEVITICUS 23–27

Continuing in Holiness

*I will walk among you and be your God, and
you will be my people.*

LEVITICUS 26:12

1. If you and your family were Israelites who lived
   in the time of Moses, which details in these
   chapters would be of most interest to you?

   _____

   _____

   _____

   _____

2. From each of the following passages in
   Leviticus 23, summarize the most important
   teachings given here regarding the celebration
   times ordained for God's people:

   Sabbath (23:3)

   _____

   _____

   _____

   _____

   _____

Optional Application: In order to better please God in our personal and corporate worship, what can we learn from Leviticus 23?

For Further Study: Compare the instructions for feasts in Leviticus 23 with those given earlier in Exodus: Passover (see Exodus 12:1-14); Feast of Unleavened Bread (see Exodus 12:15-20; 13:3-10; 23:15; 34:18); Feast of Weeks, or Feast of Harvest (see Exodus 23:16; 34:22); Feast of Tabernacles, or Feast of Booths or Feast of Ingathering (see Exodus 23:16; 34:22).

Passover and Feast of Unleavened Bread (23:4-8)

_____

_____

_____

_____

Feast of Firstfruits (23:9-14)

_____

_____

_____

_____

Feast of Weeks (23:15-22)

_____

_____

_____

_____

Feast of Trumpets (23:23-25)

_____

_____

_____

_____

Day of Atonement (23:26-32)

_____

_____

_____

_____

Feast of Tabernacles, or Feast of Booths
(23:33-43)

_____

_____

_____

For Thought and Discussion: What emotions do you think God Himself may have been experiencing during the events of the last half of Leviticus 24?

Optional Application: What do you learn most about God's character and personality in Leviticus 24, and what does it mean personally for you at this time?

3. From what you see in chapter 23, how would you describe the *beauty* of the celebrations commanded there?

praise + thankfulness to the Lord for everything the Israelites had.

4. What is the significance of the oil lamps and bread set before the Lord in Leviticus 24:1-9?

to show lasting covenant for future generations. reminder of daily activities in tabernacle

5. Summarize the events recorded in 24:10-23, as well as God's response and the regulations He gave.

Anyone who blasphemes the Lord, takes the life of a human being, animal, — Gods response put to death restitution for killing someones animal. If he injures another they must be injured the same way. eye for eye etc.

6. Summarize the instructions God gave in 25:1-7 for the Sabbath Year and His intention behind those instructions.

Rest the land 7th year — do no work on your land during the 7th year

_____

65

7. From 25:8-22, summarize God's instructions and promises regarding the Year of Jubilee and His intention behind them.

49 yrs. 10th day of 7th month, day of atonement 50 yr; jubilee – do not sow or eat of the fields

8. From 25:23-34, summarize God's regulations for property redemption, and explain their significance and intent.

The lands will be returned to owner in yr. of jubilee relative could come Christ come as our redeemer

9. From 25:35-55, summarize God's regulations regarding the poor, and explain the underlying moral principles and values.

help those in need (the poor) + let him live among you. – Because the Israelites are God's servants. treat slaves properly.

10. From chapter 26, summarize the blessings that are promised to Israel for obeying God and the punishment that is promised for their disobedience.

God blessed all Israelites to encourage obedience + peace. Punishment 7 times - soil + trees will not bear crops + He will send wild animals against you.

peace + crops

11. In chapter 26, notice God's emphasis on Himself in verses 24 and 28. What does He want His people to deeply understand about Himself? (Relate this in your own words.)

He saved His people + loves
them + they will prosper only
if they obey.

For Further Study: Examine Deuteronomy 28 to determine how closely it parallels Leviticus 26.

"The nation is reminded that all God's promises, of good harvests, peace, and his own presence, will be theirs if they observe his commandments. But if they forget his word and go their own way, they will experience all those things that men fear most: sickness, drought, death of children, famine, enemy occupation, and deportation to foreign lands. Leviticus stresses that if such a fate befalls Israel, it will not be in spite of the covenant but because of it. God himself will punish his disobedient people."[1]

12. In 26:14-39, notice the repeating pattern of God's discipline and correction, followed by the people's disobedience. Can this pattern be broken? If so, how? If not, why not?

_____

_____

_____

_____

13. How do you see God's *grace* emphasized in 26:40-45?

God is slow to anger + gives
them opportunities to repent.
He did not want to destroy
them.

"Divine blessing depends on obedience, but disobedience will not result in total rejection, just continued divine judgment."[2]

14. From Leviticus 27, summarize God's regulations about vows, and explain their significance and intent.

   Whatever they promised to the Lord must be obeyed. They could not go back on their word.

15. As this book concludes, what would you say are the greatest challenges or potential dangers facing the people of Israel at this time?

16. What are the most important ways in which you see God's *grace* throughout these closing chapters of Leviticus?

17. What would you select as the key verse or passage in Leviticus 23–27—the passage that best captures or reflects the dynamics of what these chapters are all about?

18. What would have been the special significance of these chapters for Israel in particular as they faced a long journey across the wilderness and a new national existence in the Promised Land?

_____

_____

_____

19. List any lingering questions you have about Leviticus 23–27.

_____

_____

_____

_____

For Thought and Discussion: How much would you agree or disagree with this statement: The most accurate definition for sin is that it's *a violation of God's laws.*

Reviewing Leviticus

20. In Romans 7:12, Paul said that God's commandments are "holy, righteous and good." What significant evidence for that assessment have you seen in Leviticus?

God doesn't command
anything unreasonable.

_____

_____

21. How does Leviticus emphasize God's hatred of sin?

thru punishments
(7 times)

_____

_____

Optional
Application: In light
of how you're doing
spiritually at this time
in your life, what
teachings in Leviticus
are most important
and helpful for you
personally, and why?

22. Jesus said in Matthew 5:18 that not even the
    least portion of God's Word "will by any means
    disappear from the Law until everything is
    accomplished." What do you think God's laws
    in Leviticus are meant to accomplish or fulfill?
    How much has already been done? How much,
    if any, is still unfinished?

1. _forgiveness — day of atonement_

2. _same_

3. _we're still sinners_

23. In your understanding, what are the strongest
    ways in which Leviticus points us to mankind's
    need for Jesus and what He accomplished in His
    death and resurrection?

we can never be fully
forgiven without Jesus.

24. Recall the guidelines given for our thought life
    in Philippians 4:8: "Whatever is true, whatever
    is noble, whatever is right, whatever is pure,
    whatever is lovely, whatever is admirable — if
    anything is excellent or praiseworthy — *think
    about such things*" (emphasis added). As
    you reflect on all you've read in the book of
    Leviticus, what stands out to you as being par-
    ticularly *true, noble, right, pure, lovely, admira-
    ble, excellent,* or *praiseworthy* — and therefore
    well worth thinking more about?

day of atonement
an angry God can
still forgive.

25. In Isaiah 55:10-11, God reminds us that in the
    same way He sends rain and snow from the
    sky to water the earth and nurture life, so also
    He sends His words to accomplish specific
    purposes. What would you suggest are God's
    primary purposes for the message of Leviticus
    in the lives of His people today?

    faith, trust, believe

26. In Romans 15:4, Paul reminded us that the Old
    Testament Scriptures can give us patience and
    perseverance on one hand, as well as comfort
    and encouragement on the other. In your own
    life, how do you see the book of Leviticus living
    up to Paul's description? In what ways does it
    help to meet your personal needs for both per-
    severance and encouragement?

    service

27. What is the best evidence you've seen in
    Leviticus that God truly loves His people?

    *an angry God can
    still forgive*

For the Group

You may want to focus your discussion for lesson 6
especially on the following issues, themes, and concepts. (These will likely reflect what group members
have learned in their individual study of this week's

passage, though they'll also have made discoveries in other areas as well.)

- Appropriate worship of God
- Corporate celebration for God's people
- The meaning and seriousness of blasphemy
- Our stewardship of the earth
- Justice and love in our relationships with others
- Rewards for obedience, punishment for disobedience
- The meaning of redemption

The following numbered questions in lesson 6 may stimulate your best and most helpful discussion: 1, 3, 12, 15, 16, 17, 18, and 19.

Allow enough discussion time to look back together and review all of Leviticus as a whole. You can use questions 22–27 in this lesson to help you do that.

Once more, look also at the questions in the margin under the heading "For Thought and Discussion."

1. Gordon J. Wenham, "The Book of Leviticus," in *The New International Commentary on the Old Testament*, vol. 3 (Grand Rapids, MI: Eerdmans, 1979), 31.
2. Wenham, 32.

THE BOOK OF NUMBERS
The Faithfulness of Our Covenant God

The book of Numbers wraps up a long and eventful stretch of time spent by the people of Israel near Mount Sinai, where God prepared them for entering the Promised Land. This preparation occupies fifty-nine consecutive chapters in Scripture — the final twenty-two in Exodus, all twenty-seven in Leviticus, and the first ten in Numbers. Finally, in Numbers 10, God's people leave Sinai, expecting shortly to enter and possess the Promised Land. But because of grievous realities emerging about themselves — and the resulting further lessons they need to learn from God — their journey is sidetracked. It stretches to four decades spent in the wilderness.

The book of Numbers vividly portrays this tragedy, along with the overriding compassion and faithfulness of God that assure His people a future of blessing, in spite of their sinful shortcomings.

"This portrayal of God's covenant faithfulness is in sharp contrast with the book's repeated depiction of human faithlessness, the utter failure of humanity to meet God's standards by its own strength. Human failures are clearly portrayed and contrasted with the wise measures of the ever-faithful covenant God."[1]

An Appropriate Name

The name "Numbers" for this book goes back to ancient times, reflecting the census counts in chapters 1 and 26, which divide the book into two parts — each one focusing on a separate generation.

"The Book of Numbers is just that! It is a book that uses numbers to celebrate the work of the Lord. And in these numbers is his praise."[2]

In Hebrew tradition, the book was also given a title reflecting the phrase "in the desert" (or "in the wilderness") in the opening verse of chapter 1.

A Book of Dramatic Variety

The content in Numbers is extremely varied, with all kinds of features that catch our attention. It also at times seems scattered in focus.

"The materials in Numbers seem to present themselves in an amazing, almost incoherent, variety. The book contains numerous lists of names and numbers, involved genealogies, dramatic historical narratives, arcane rites of purification and ritual sacrifice, lists of sites visited in the wanderings of Israel, lovely poetry, the quintessential blessing of the Lord on his people, impassioned personal encounters, rather dull and prosaic documents on priestly duties, engaging flashes of personality conflicts, stories of intrigue and betrayal, accounts of robust heroism and daring faith, tedious descriptions of detail in ritual, some hymn fragments, quotations from other ancient books, exultant praises to God, and—most surprisingly—exalted poetic prophecies providing a blessing of Israel from a pagan mantic prophet who has fallen under the 'spell' of the God of Israel."[3]

This variety reflects the richness of the revelation God makes about Himself in this book. "The ultimate source of most of the material in Numbers is divine. Nearly every section begins 'The LORD spoke to Moses' or with some similar remark."[4]

For Our Worship

Numbers also brings us a wider and deeper perspective on our approach to the sovereign and faithful God. "The theme of the Book of Numbers is worship. . . . The pulse of the book is worship. It *is* the worship of God by Moses and those who align themselves with him. By God's grace it may become a book of worship for us as well."[5]

This thrust toward worship is reflected especially in the highlighted themes of God's presence and holiness, as well as His graciousness and faithfulness. All these come together in Numbers to draw us toward our Creator and Redeemer in praise and thanksgiving.

Timeline: From Egypt to the Promised Land[6]

The "first month" and "first year" as reckoned in Numbers are established according to the time when the Israelites left Egypt, immediately following the original Passover and the plague on the Egyptian firstborn (see Exodus 12:1-2).

Year	Month	Day(s)	Events	Text
1 (ca. 1446 BC)	1	10–14	Israelites observe the first Passover in Egypt	Exodus 12:1-6,28
1	1	15	Israelites set out from Rameses in Egypt	Numbers 33:3-5; Exodus 12:37
2	1–3		Israelites journey out of Egypt, across the Red Sea, and on to Mount Sinai	Numbers 33:5-15; Exodus 13:17–19:2
2	1	1	(at Sinai:) completion of tabernacle; laws for offerings begin; offerings for altar begin; ordination of priests begins	Numbers 7:1 (with Exodus 40:2,17); Numbers 7:3; Leviticus 1:1; 8:1
2	1	8	(at Sinai:) ordination of priests completed	Leviticus 9:1
2	1	12	(at Sinai:) offerings for altar completed; appointment of Levites	Numbers 7:38; 8:5
2	1	14	(at Sinai:) second Passover observed	Numbers 9:2
2	2	1	(at Sinai:) census begins	Numbers 1:1
2	2	14	(at Sinai:) Passover for those unclean	Numbers 9:11
2	2	20	(at Sinai:) the cloud moves; the camp begins its trek	Numbers 10:11-28; 33:16
2			(at Hazeroth:) Miriam and Aaron oppose Moses	Numbers 11:35; 12:1-15; 33:17

1. *New Geneva Study Bible* (Nashville: Thomas Nelson, 1995), introduction to Numbers: "Characteristics and Themes."
2. Ronald B. Allen, "Numbers," in *The Expositor's Bible Commentary*, vol. 2, ed. Frank E. Gaebelein (Grand Rapids, MI: Zondervan, 1990), 691.
3. Allen, 670.
4. Gordon J. Wenham, "Numbers: An Introduction and Commentary," in the *Tyndale Old Testament Commentaries*, vol. 4, ed. D. J. Wiseman (Downers Grove, IL: InterVarsity, 1981), 21.
5. Allen, 658.
6. Timeline adapted from these sources: (1) table on page 757 in Ronald B. Allen's "Numbers," in *The Expositors Bible Commentary*, vol. 2, ed. Frank E. Gaebelein (Grand Rapids, MI: Zondervan, 1990); and (2) tables on pages 103 and 245 in Gordon J. Wenham's "Numbers: An Introduction and Commentary," in the *Tyndale Old Testament Commentaries*, vol. 4, ed. D. J. Wiseman (Downers Grove, IL: InterVarsity, 1981).

LESSON SEVEN

NUMBERS 1–6
A Mighty Host

*All the Israelites twenty years old or more who
were able to serve in Israel's army were counted
according to their families. The total number
was 603,550.*

NUMBERS 1:45-46

1. Once more, think about the encouraging guidelines in 2 Timothy 3:16-17 — that *all* Scripture
   is of great benefit to (a) teach us, (b) rebuke us,
   (c) correct us, and (d) train us in righteousness,
   and that it will completely equip the person of
   God "for every good work." Give serious con-
   sideration to these guidelines. In which of these
   areas do you especially want to experience the
   usefulness of Numbers? Express your desire in a
   written prayer to God.

   _____

   _____

   _____

   _____

2. Recall again how God says His Word is like fire
   and like a hammer (see Jeremiah 23:29). He can
   use His Word to burn away unclean thoughts
   and desires in our hearts. He can use it with
   hammer-like hardness to crush and crumble
   our spiritual hardness. From your study of
   Numbers, how do you most want to see the

77

Optional Application: After His resurrection, when Jesus was explaining Old Testament passages to His disciples, we read that He "opened their minds so they could understand the Scriptures" (Luke 24:45). Ask God to do that kind of work in *your* mind as you study Numbers so you're released and free to learn everything here He wants you to learn and so you can become as bold and worshipful and faithful as those early disciples of Jesus were. Express this desire to Him in prayer.

For Thought and Discussion: As you launch into a closer look at Numbers, how would you summarize what you already know about this book? And how would you describe the general impression most Christians have of it?

"fire-and-hammer" power of God's Word at work in your life? Express this longing in a written prayer to God.

_____

_____

_____

_____

3. Think again about 2 Timothy 2:15: "Do your best to present yourself to God as one approved, a worker who does not need to be ashamed and who correctly handles the word of truth." Getting the most from your study will take concentration and perseverance. Express here your commitment before God to work diligently as you study Numbers, that you may "present yourself to God as one approved."

_____

_____

_____

_____

The Lord spoke to Moses (1:1). This opening phrase is repeated often in Numbers, just as it is in Leviticus. Notice the majestic repetition of this phrase in Numbers at the beginning of chapters 2, 4–6, 8–10, 13, 15, 17–19, 26, 28, 31, 34–35 and also at 3:5,40; 4:17,21; 5:5,11; 6:22; 8:5,23; 9:9; 11:16; 14:11,26; 15:17,37; 16:20,36; 18:25; 20:12; 21:8,16,34; 25:4,10,16; 26:52; 27:12,18; 31:25; 33:50; 34:16; 35:9. Take note of the natural divisions this repeated phrase marks in the text.

4. In chapter 1, how do the details regarding the census emphasize that Israel is to be battle-minded and combat-ready?

_____

_____

_____

_____

The numbers mentioned in the census of
Numbers 1 and the census of Numbers 26 are
often considered unrealistically high by schol-
ars and historians, although they have reached
no consensus about how and why these numbers might be inflated.

For Thought and Discussion: The census in Numbers 1 counts men who can go to war "able to serve in the army" (1:3), a phrase used thirteen times in this chapter. Do God's people today need to have a similar mind-set for battle-readiness? If so, in what ways?

5. In 1:47-54, how is the special status and work of the tribe of Levi brought out?

_____

_____

_____

6. How does the first chapter in Numbers reflect Israel's preparation for the conquest of the Promised Land?

_____

_____

_____

7. In the arrangement for Israel's camp (see chapter 2), what are the major features, and what do you see as their significance?

_____

_____

_____

_____

8. How does chapter 2 reflect Israel's preparation for the conquest of the Promised Land?

_____

For Further Study:
Review Exodus 28–29
to better understand
the special obliga-
tions and privileges
accorded to Aaron
and his sons. How
would you summarize
the essence of their
responsibilities and
status?

9. How do the words of 3:1-4 reinforce the special
holiness of the Aaronic priesthood (which we've
seen earlier in Exodus and Leviticus)?

10. In 3:5-39, what were the specific duties given
to the Levites as a whole and to their various
clans?

The chief leader of the Levites was Eleazar
(3:32). See the description of his duties in 4:16
and 19:2-5. Eleazar will go on to play a promi-
nent role in Numbers and will succeed to the
priestly office of his father, Aaron. See 16:37-
40; 20:23-28; 26:1-3.

11. What do we learn in 3:11-13 and 3:40-51 about
the special condition of the firstborn sons in
Israel and about God's provision in that regard?

12. How does chapter 3 relate to Israel's preparation for the conquest of the Promised Land?

_____

_____

_____

13. From chapter 4, how would you summarize . . .

a. the tasks of the Kohathites (verses 1-20)?

_____

_____

_____

b. the tasks of the Gershonites (verses 21-28)?

_____

_____

_____

c. the tasks of the Merarites (verses 29-33)?

_____

_____

_____

14. How does chapter 4 relate to Israel's preparation for the conquest of the Promised Land?

_____

_____

_____

15. In chapter 5, how is God's holiness emphasized, as well as His requirements for His people's holiness?

_____

_____

_____

16. What underlying moral principles and values do you see behind the regulations in Numbers 5?

_____

_____

_____

_____

17. How does chapter 5 relate to Israel's preparation for the conquest of the Promised Land?

_____

_____

_____

18. From 6:1-21, summarize the special requirements and obligations of those who took a Nazirite vow.

_____

_____

_____

_____

A special vow (6:2). "This vow . . . does not describe a routine matter or even an expected act of devotion one might make from time to time. It is an act of unusual devotion to God, based perhaps on an intense desire to demonstrate to the Lord one's utter separation to him."[1]

Dedication to the LORD (6:2). "This is where the text lays its primary stress; the prohibitions were means of achieving the sense of separation. The Nazirite vow was not just an act of superior self-discipline, an achieving of a spiritual machismo; it was to be regarded as a supreme act of total devotion to the person and work of the Lord that would override certain normal and expected patterns of behavior."[2]

19. What does the blessing in 6:22-27 communicate to us about God and His desire for His people?

_____

_____

_____

_____

20. How do you see Jesus Christ as being the fulfillment and the assurance to us of all the gifts in Numbers 6:24-26?

God's blessing of you

_____

_____

_____

His guarding you and keeping you

_____

_____

_____

His face shining upon you

_____

_____

_____

His grace

_____

_____

_____

His face turned toward you

_____

_____

For Further Study:
Reflect again on the beautiful blessing given in 6:24-26. How do the following passages deepen the meaning of the different parts of this blessing?

- "the LORD bless you": Genesis 28:3-4; Luke 24:50-51

- "and keep you": Psalms 91:11; 121:3-8; Isaiah 42:6; John 17:11; 1 Thessalonians 5:23; Jude 24

- "the LORD make his face shine upon you": Psalms 31:16; 80:7; 119:135; 2 Corinthians 4:6

- "and be gracious to you": John 1:16-17; 2 Corinthians 13:14; Ephesians 6:24; Philippians 4:23; 2 Peter 1:2-3

- "the LORD turn his face toward you": Psalms 4:6; 89:15

- "and give you peace": Psalm 29:11; Isaiah 26:3,12; Luke 2:14; John 14:27; 16:33; 20:21-22; Romans 5:1; 15:13; Philippians 4:7

Optional Application: Knowing that Numbers 6:22-27 states God's desire for your well-being in Christ, thank Him for these gifts and express to Him your desire for more of each one: His blessing you, His keeping you, His face shining upon you, His grace to you, His face turned toward you, and His peace.

Optional Application: How can you seek the blessings of Numbers 6:24-26 for others?

His peace

_____

_____

_____

21. How does chapter 6 relate to Israel's preparation for the conquest of the Promised Land?

_____

_____

_____

22. What would you select as the key verse or passage in Numbers 1–6 — one that best captures or reflects the dynamics of what these chapters are all about?

_____

_____

_____

23. List any lingering questions you have about Numbers 1–6.

_____

_____

_____

_____

For the Group

You may want to focus your discussion for lesson 7 especially on the following issues, themes, and concepts. (These things will likely reflect what group members have learned in their individual study of this week's passage, though they'll also have made discoveries in other areas as well.)

- Being holy and clean in God's sight
- Completeness and wholeness in God's sight
- The meaning of consecration for service to God
- The experience of God's blessing

The following numbered questions in lesson 7 may stimulate your best and most helpful discussion: 4, 7, 15, 16, 19, 20, 22, and 23.

Look also at the questions in the margin under the heading "For Thought and Discussion."

1. Ronald B. Allen, "Numbers," in *The Expositor's Bible Commentary*, vol. 2, ed. Frank E. Gaebelein (Grand Rapids, MI: Zondervan, 1990), 749.
2. Allen, 749.

NUMBERS 7–12

The Journey Launched

*The cloud lifted from above the tabernacle of
the covenant law. Then the Israelites set out
from the Desert of Sinai and traveled from
place to place until the cloud came to rest in the
Desert of Paran.*

NUMBERS 10:11-12

When Moses finished setting up the tabernacle
(7:1). Literally, "On the day Moses finished setting up the tabernacle." According to Exodus
40:2 and 40:17, this happened on the first day
of the first month of the second year after the
Exodus from Egypt. The events beginning in
chapter 7 thus occurred a month before the
census described in chapter 1.

1. In 7:12-83, notice the twelvefold repetition in
   the description of the offerings made by the
   twelve tribes on twelve consecutive days. What
   do you learn about the reasons for these offerings in 7:1-11 and 7:84-88?

   _____

   _____

   _____

   _____

87

2. What do you see as the significance of the words about Moses in 7:89?

_____

_____

_____

See that all seven [lamps] light up the area in front of the lampstand (8:2). Discover more about these in Exodus 25:31-40 and 37:17-24.

---

3. How does Numbers 7 relate to Israel's preparation for the conquest of the Promised Land?

_____

_____

_____

4. How does the passage about the Levites in Numbers 8:5-26 build further upon the description of their duties in chapters 3 and 4?

_____

_____

_____

5. How does chapter 8 relate to Israel's preparation for the conquest of the Promised Land?

_____

_____

_____

6. What is the significance of the Passover celebration in chapter 9?

_____

_____

_____

7. From 9:15-23, what impressions do you have of God and the nature of His relationship with His people?

_____

_____

_____

_____

8. How does chapter 9 relate to Israel's preparation for the conquest of the Promised Land?

_____

_____

_____

9. What is the purpose and significance of the silver trumpets, as described in 10:1-10?

_____

_____

_____

Optional Application: What guidelines and principles for God's guidance of His people can you ascertain in Numbers 9:15-23, and how do these relate personally to you?

For Further Study: As He does in 9:15-23, how did God earlier demonstrate His guidance of the people through the fiery cloud in Exodus 13:21-22 and 40:34-38?

Optional Application: In order to better please God in our personal and corporate worship, what can we learn from Numbers 7–9?

The Israelites set out from the Desert of Sinai (10:12). Their stay at Sinai had lasted almost a year and was quite eventful, as described in Exodus 19–40, in all of Leviticus, and in the first ten chapters of Numbers. At last the people of Israel are moving again toward the Promised Land.

---

10. What is significant about the traveling procedures for the Israelites, as described in 10:11-36?

_____

_____

_____

_____

Optional Application: Can you relate to the people's complaining and craving in chapter 11? In what kinds of circumstances or situations do you find yourself being tempted toward this same reaction? What can you learn from this chapter about dealing with such temptation?

For Further Study: In 11:29, Moses stated his desire that all God's people become prophets. Compare this with the prophecy for God's people in Joel 2:28-32, with the events described in Acts 2, and with Paul's words about prophecy in 1 Corinthians 14:1-5 and 14:29-40.

11. In what specific ways does 10:11-28 correlate with the earlier instructions given in Numbers 2?

_____

_____

_____

12. How does chapter 10 in Numbers relate to Israel's preparation for the conquest of the Promised Land?

_____

_____

_____

13. Describe what we learn in 11:1-15 about the character of God's people, about His response to this, and about the response of Moses.

_____

_____

_____

_____

14. From 11:16-30, summarize the circumstances and experiences of the seventy elders appointed by Moses.

_____

_____

_____

_____

The Spirit rested on them (11:25). "When this passage (like most of the Old Testament) speaks of the work of the Spirit, it is focusing primarily on the empowering of the Spirit for service to the people of God, more than an internal, personal experience."[1]

---

15. What does the incident in 11:31-34 reveal about the character of God's people and about His response to this?

_____

_____

_____

_____

16. Describe what we learn in chapter 12 about the character of Aaron and Miriam, about God's response to this, and about the response of Moses.

_____

_____

_____

_____

A very humble man (12:3). See also the words of Jesus in Matthew 11:29.

The people . . . encamped in the Desert of Paran (12:16). This region included the location known as Kadesh or Kadesh Barnea (see Numbers 13:26; 32:8). The events in Numbers 13–19 will center around this location.

17. In Numbers 11–12, what do you see as the major lessons for the leaders of God's people?

_____

_____

_____

_____

18. Also in Numbers 11–12, what do you see as the major lessons for God's people to learn about the right response to God-appointed leadership?

Optional Application: Moses said, "I wish that all the Lord's people were prophets" (11:29), a sentiment echoed by Paul in 1 Corinthians 14:1-5. In what ways, if any, has God gifted you with prophecy for His people, in accordance with His desires for you?

Optional Application: What personal lessons in humility do you learn from Numbers 12?

For Further Study: In Numbers 11–12, how do the people's complaints, after finally leaving Sinai, compare with their complaints a year earlier on their way to Sinai, as recorded in Exodus 15:22–16:3 and 17:1-3? How do the responses of Moses and God in Numbers 11–12 compare with their responses in Exodus 15–17?

_____

_____

_____

19. What would you select as the key verse or pas-
    sage in Numbers 7–12 — one that best captures
    or reflects the dynamics of what these chapters
    are all about?

_____

_____

_____

20. List any lingering questions you have about
    Numbers 7–12.

_____

_____

_____

_____

For the Group

You may want to focus your discussion for lesson 8
especially on the following issues, themes, and concepts. (These will likely reflect what group members
have learned in their individual study of this week's
passage, though they'll also have made discoveries
in other areas as well.)

- Appropriate worship of God
- Contentment
- Humility

The following numbered questions in lesson 8
may stimulate your best and most helpful discussion: 2, 5, 6, 7, 13, 14, 15, 17, 18, 19, and 20.
Look also at the questions in the margin under
the heading "For Thought and Discussion."

1. *ESV Study Bible* (Wheaton, IL: Crossway, 2008), at
   Numbers 11:24-30.

NUMBERS 13–19

Crisis and Calamity

How long will these people treat me with contempt? How long will they refuse to believe in me, in spite of all the miraculous signs I have performed among them?

NUMBERS 14:11

For Thought and Discussion: What are the most important qualities that can help a leader motivate people in difficult circumstances?

The events of these chapters include the generation-long wandering by the people in the wilderness, a result of God's judgment on their rebellion following the evil report of the spies in Numbers 13–14.

1. Describe the specific mission given in 13:1-24 to the twelve spies and their experiences in carrying this out.

_____

_____

_____

_____

2. What are the most important details in the account of the report given by the spies and its conflicting interpretations (see 13:25-33)?

_____

_____

_____

Optional Application: Can you relate to the people's negative reactions in 14:1-4, especially in relation to challenging circumstances that God leads you into? If you sometimes are tempted to share those negative reactions, what can you learn from this passage about dealing with them?

For Thought and Discussion: What are the most potent kinds of fear that keep people from boldly going forward in the face of adversity?

3. What explanation can you give for the people's response in 14:1-4?

4. Chapter 14 has been called the key to the book of Numbers. Why might this be so?

5. Describe in detail what we learn in chapter 14 about the character of God's people, about His response to this, and about the responses of Moses and Aaron.

"Marking as it does the collapse of the national plan, and the postponement of God's promises to the patriarchs, the incident of the spies is more than just another example of Israel's rebellion in the wilderness. It is a historical watershed. Here the final break with Egypt is made. Those who yearned for the luxuries of Egyptian slavery die in the desert; their children, chastened by their wilderness experiences, enter the promised land."[1]

6. How would you evaluate the psychological condition of the people as represented in the various things happening in chapters 13 and 14?

_____

_____

_____

_____

Optional Application: What lessons in prayer and intercession can you learn from Moses in Numbers 14:13-19?

They will meet their end in this wilderness; here they will die (14:35). Because of this judgment from God, Israel's entry into the Promised Land was delayed until forty years after the Exodus from Egypt. Yet little is said about what happened to the people during these decades in the desert. (Numbers 20 apparently jumps forward to the fortieth year after the Exodus.)

"The larger part of the sojourn in the desert is left without record. This may be deliberate on Moses' part. It is as though the time of sojourn was time that did not really count in the history of salvation. . . . We are left to ourselves to try to imagine what it was like for the people during this long, dreary time in the desert."[2]

7. In chapter 15, what is significant about these laws being placed immediately after the account of the tragic events in chapters 13–14?

_____

_____

_____

8. How do the laws for sacrifices described in 15:1-16 compare with what you have learned about these things in Leviticus 1–7?

For Further Study:
In 15:1-16, how is your understanding of these laws deepened by what you read in Genesis 18:1-8 and Psalm 50:12-15?

9. How does the offering described in 15:17-21 build on what you have read in Leviticus 19:24-25 and 23:10-11?

10. How do the laws in 15:22-31 compare with what you have learned about sacrifices for unintentional sins in Leviticus 4–5?

"The sacrificial offerings . . . are no longer valid expressions of Christian worship, because they point beyond themselves to the one atoning sacrifice of Christ which has made them obsolete (Hebrews 10). Yet Christians are still reminded: 'let us continually offer to God a sacrifice of praise — the fruit of lips that openly profess his name. And do not forget to do good and to share with others, for with such sacrifices God is pleased' (Hebrews 13:15-16). The principle of wholehearted dedication to the worship of God links Old and New Testaments, even if our mode of devotion has altered. . . . If much of the biblical legislation cannot be applied today, its thoroughness and attention to detail should challenge the modern church to ask whether our more casual attitudes may not be a cloak for indifference."[3]

11. What do we learn about God's holiness in the incident described in 15:32-36?

_____

_____

_____

_____

12. What is the significance of the regulations mentioned in 15:37-41?

_____

_____

_____

_____

13. From 16:1-35, list the most significant details involved in Korah's rebellion and in God's response through Moses and Aaron.

_____

_____

_____

_____

"There is no indication how long after the spies' return Korah mounted his rebellion. The events described [in Numbers 16] may have taken place at any time within the thirty-eight years the Israelites spent wandering in the wilderness near Kadesh."[4]

For Further Study: From your earlier study in Leviticus, what passages in that book are echoed in the words of Numbers 15:40-41? How does this repetition reinforce the significance of these truths?

Optional Application: In order to better please God in our personal and corporate worship, what can we learn from His words to Israel in Numbers 15?

Optional Application: In what ways do you share an obligation to conform your life to what God says in Numbers 15:39-41? Ask God for His guidance and help in this. What specific action should you take immediately? And what "tassels" do you need as reminders?

God who gives breath to all living things (16:22).
This phrase — in the desperate prayer Moses
and Aaron make after Korah's rebellion
grows — is used elsewhere only in Moses'
prayer in 27:16.

14. What is significant about Eleazar's actions in
    16:36-40?

    _____

    _____

    _____

15. What do we learn in 16:41-50 about the charac-
    ter of God's people, about His response to this,
    and about the responses of Moses and Aaron?

    _____

    _____

    _____

    _____

16. What is significant about the events recorded in
    chapter 17, and how do they relate to what hap-
    pened in chapter 16?

    _____

    _____

    _____

17. What would you summarize as the most impor-
    tant leadership lessons given in chapters 16–17,
    especially in regard to leading God's people?

    _____

    _____

    _____

    _____

18. How does chapter 18 reinforce the special responsibilities and privileges of the Aaronic priesthood?

_____

_____

_____

_____

19. Summarize the regulations for purification given in chapter 19, and explain their significance.

_____

_____

_____

_____

20. What would you select as the key verse or passage in Numbers 13–19 — one that best captures or reflects the dynamics of what these chapters are all about?

_____

_____

_____

21. List any lingering questions you have about Numbers 13–19.

_____

_____

_____

_____

Optional Application: How would you evaluate the quality of your own submission to the leaders God has appointed over His people? What further action or commitment in this area is needed on your part?

For Further Study: How does the description of the priesthood in Numbers 18 deepen the meaning of our calling today as priests? As you answer this, recall 1 Peter 2:9 ("You are . . . a royal priesthood"), and look closely at Revelation 1:6, 5:10, and 20:6.

For the Group

You may want to focus your discussion for lesson 9 especially on the following issues, themes, and concepts. (These will likely reflect what group members have learned in their individual study of this week's passage, though they'll also have made discoveries in other areas as well.)

- Trust in God's guidance
- Courage and endurance in facing challenges and adversity
- Leadership among God's people
- Cleanness and holiness before the Lord

The following numbered questions in lesson 9 may stimulate your best and most helpful discussion: 1, 4, 5, 6, 11, 13, 15, 17, 20, and 21.

Remember to look also at the "For Thought and Discussion" questions in the margin.

1. Gordon J. Wenham, "Numbers: An Introduction and Commentary," in the *Tyndale Old Testament Commentaries*, vol. 4, ed. D. J. Wiseman (Downers Grove, IL: InterVarsity, 1981), 130.
2. Ronald B. Allen, "Numbers," in *The Expositor's Bible Commentary*, vol. 2, ed. Frank E. Gaebelein (Grand Rapids, MI: Zondervan, 1990), 866.
3. Wenham, 59.
4. Wenham, 150.

NUMBERS 20–25

Drama on the Plains of Moab

I see him, but not now; I behold him, but not near. A star will come out of Jacob; a scepter will rise out of Israel.

NUMBERS 24:17

1. Remember again the picture we're given in Proverbs 2:1-5: the person who truly longs for wisdom and understanding will search the Scriptures for it as if there were treasure buried there and will come to understand the fear of the Lord and discover the knowledge of God. As you continue exploring Numbers, what "hidden treasure" would you like God to help you find here—to show you what God and His wisdom are really like? If you have this desire, how would you express it in a prayer to God?

_____

_____

_____

_____

In the first month (20:1). This is generally thought to be the first month in the fortieth year after Israel left Egypt, or thirty-eight years after the events recorded at the beginning of Numbers. This chapter goes on to record the death of Aaron, and 33:38 indicates that this occurred in the fortieth year.

At the Desert of Zin . . . at Kadesh (20:1). The Israelites were at Kadesh Barnea earlier, when the spies brought back their fearful report and the people rebelled. The mention of this location here may indicate that the Israelites returned to Kadesh after many years of wandering nearby, or it may recall their earlier encampment at Kadesh. The phrase might be "a narrator's device designed to take us back into the narrative story line by the use of recall. . . . It is as though the narrator were to say, 'Now you will recall that the nation had moved to the Desert of Zin and had dwelled for a lengthy period at Kadesh.'"[1]

Chapter 20 records the deaths of both Miriam (verse 1) and Aaron (verse 28), as well as the sin Moses commits (verses 10-12), which will ultimately bring death to him also before he can enter the Promised Land (as God will later explain to him, in 27:12-14).

"Here is the passing of the noblest of the leadership of the people, the old guard. Those whom God had used to establish the nation were dying before the nation came into its own. Miriam who had led the joyful singing at the day of redemption (Exodus 15) would not live to sing a song of praise to the Lord in Canaan. Aaron who had led the people for a generation in the worship of sacrifice of untold numbers of animals would not be allowed to offer a tiny pigeon in the Promised Land. And Moses, hoary old man that he was — a life that cannot be rivaled in the service of God save only in the life of Jesus — Moses, who spoke the words of God from the holy mount of Sinai, would see the Promised Land only from a promontory in Moab."[2]

2. Describe what we learn in 20:2-13 about the character of God's people, about the character of Moses, and about God's view of all this.

_____

_____

_____

_____

3. How does this generation's complaints along their journey — as seen in 20:2-5 and 21:4-5 — compare with those of the previous generation in Numbers 11–12?

_____

_____

_____

_____

4. What is significant about Edom's refusal to allow Israel to pass through their land (see 20:14-21)?

_____

_____

_____

_____

For Thought and Discussion: What is it about complaining that can have such a negative impact on work and service?

For Further Study: How does Philippians 2:14-15 speak to the kinds of attitudes God's people displayed in Numbers 20:2-5 and 21:4-5?

Optional Application: In what situations are you most tempted to be a complainer? What can you learn from these chapters in Numbers about dealing with that temptation?

Edom (20:14). See Genesis 25:24-26 and 33:1-17. The Edomites were the people most closely related to the people of Israel.

For Further Study:
In John 3:14-15, see
how Jesus applied to
Himself the story of
the serpent raised on
a pole by Moses.

For Further Study:
Read 2 Kings 18:4 to
discover what hap-
pened centuries later
to the snake on the
pole made by Moses.

**Optional
Application:** Do
you have a share in
any sin that's like the
one God judges so
severely in Numbers
21:4-9? In whatever
you identify regard-
ing this, confess it
before the Lord.

5. What is significant about the victory over the Canaanites reported in Numbers 21:1-3?

_____

_____

_____

6. Describe what we learn in 21:4-9 about the character of God's people and about His response to this.

_____

_____

_____

_____

A bronze snake (21:9), or *a copper snake* (21:9, NIV margin). "The Hebrew term translated 'bronze' can also mean 'copper.' . . . The area through which the Israelites were traveling had copper mines, and archaeologists have found a 5-inch-long (13 cm) copper snake in a Midianite shrine at Timna, so it seems likely that copper is meant here. The redness of copper suggested atonement (see 19:1-10), so symbolically it was well chosen for this occasion."[3]

---

7. What significance do you see in Israel's victories recorded in 21:21-30?

_____

_____

_____

8. What are the most surprising details to you in the extended story of Balak and Balaam in chapters 22–24?

_____

_____

For Further Study:
In Joshua 2:10 and 9:9-10, note how Israel's victories over Sihon and Og had gained fame among other nations. See also how Israel remembered and celebrated these victories in Deuteronomy 2:24–3:11; 29:7; 31:4; Joshua 12:1-6; Judges 11:19-22; Nehemiah 9:22; Psalms 135:8-12; 136:17-21. Why do you think these victories made such a deep impression on Israel's national consciousness?

"In one of the most remarkable sections of the Bible, the Lord worked providentially and directly to proclaim his continued faithfulness to his people, despite their continuing unfaithfulness. This section is the comic account of Balaam the pagan diviner (Numbers 22–24). Here the God of laughter brings a smile to his people to encourage them in the prospects of their new hope, even as the older persons among them were still dying: God's promises will still be realized . . . in us!"[4]

"The charming naivety of these stories disguises a brilliance of literary composition and a profundity of theological reflection. The narrative is at once both very funny and deadly serious."[5]

9. In chapter 22, what desires and motivations are at work in Balak and Balaam, and what actions do these lead to?

_____

_____

_____

_____

10. What discoveries does Balaam make in chapter 22?

_____

_____

_____

_____

> The episode of Balaam's talking donkey (22:28-30) "prepares the reader to accept the validity of Balaam's oracles despite his foreign background. If God can open a donkey's eyes to an angel and enable it to speak, how much more easily can the Spirit of God enlighten heathen Balaam and put true words into his mouth (22:28, 38; 23:5, 12, 16; 24:2)."[6]

Do only what I tell you (22:20). See also 23:3, 12,16,26; 24:13.

"The theological importance of the Balaam episode is revealed by the length and detail in which the events are described. The repeated insistence in the narrative that Balaam will say only what God tells him focuses our attention on the oracles. What did the Spirit have to announce through Balaam?"[7]

11. For Balaam's first two oracles, summarize the relevant circumstances behind his speaking as well as the substance of what he spoke.

first oracle (23:1-12)

_____

_____

_____

_____

second oracle (23:13-30)

_____

_____

_____

_____

12. In Numbers 23:19, what is significant about the way Balaam affirms God's truthfulness and integrity?

_____

_____

_____

"Balaam is himself a foil for God. Balaam is constantly shifting, prevaricating, equivocating, changing — he is himself the prime example of the distinction between God and man. . . . Balaam's view of gods was based on his own human failings. Now he confronts God who is not like man in his failures at all. This is the stunning reality. All others may change; God — even with all his power — cannot change, for he cannot deny himself (cf. 1 Samuel 15:29; Psalm 89:35-37). God must fulfill his promise, for he has bound his character to his word."[8]

13. For Balaam's third oracle (24:1-9), summarize the relevant circumstances behind his speaking as well as the substance of what he spoke.

_____

_____

_____

For Further Study:
How do Balaam's first
three oracles con-
firm God's words to
Abraham in Genesis
12:2-3 and 13:16?

The Spirit of God came on him (24:2). "This time
there is a significant change. Balaam does not
go about his normal routine of sorcery (v.1).
This time 'the Spirit of God came on him' (v.2).
This unexpected language is used to prepare
the reader for the heightened revelation that is
about to come from the unwitting messenger.
The oracles are building in intensity and in
their depth of meaning."[9]

14. What are the dominant impressions of Israel
that come through in Balaam's first three oracles? What is God communicating most about
His people here?

_____

_____

_____

_____

15. How would you describe Balaam and Barak's
reactions to these first three oracles, as indicated in 24:10-14?

_____

_____

_____

Let me warn you of . . . days to come (24:14).
"The oracles could well have ended with the
great third word from Balaam. But they do
not end; there is one grander yet to come. . . .
Balaam . . . is constrained by the Lord to speak
again, his greatest oracle. In the phrase 'in days
to come' we recognize the signal in biblical literature for the distant future."[10]

16. For Balaam's fourth oracle (24:15-19), summarize the essence of what he spoke.

_____

_____

_____

I see him . . . I behold him. . . . A star will come out of Jacob; a scepter will rise out of Israel (24:17). "Perhaps fulfilled initially in David, but ultimately in the coming Messianic ruler. Israel's future Deliverer will be like a star (cf. Revelation 22:16) and scepter in his royalty and will bring victory over the enemies of his people (see v.19)."[11]

"This text [24:17] speaks unmistakably of the coming of the Messiah. That this prophecy should come from one who was unworthy makes the prophecy all the more dramatic and startling. . . . Balaam was unworthy of the words that passed through his lips, even as others were unworthy of the role they played in the salvation history of the Bible. But the words were not compromised; it was the Spirit who gave him utterance (v.2). It was also the Spirit who directed the process that led to these words being included in the Torah of God."[12]

17. In 24:20-24, how do these last shorter oracles of Balaam confirm the thought expressed in 24:17-19 that God will cause Israel's enemies to be conquered?

_____

_____

_____

For Further Study:
For a fuller picture of Balaam, look ahead to Numbers 31:9-16, Deuteronomy 23:4-5, 2 Peter 2:15, Jude 11, and Revelation 2:14.

Optional Application: How do the truths brought out in Numbers 22–24 deepen your perspective of God's people today? Give appropriate thanksgiving to God for what is eternally true about His people, from His perspective.

"There is nothing in 24:25 to prepare us for the suddenness of 25:1. . . .

"This chapter [25] presents a formative encounter with Baal worship, a miniature of the disaster that would one day engulf and destroy the nation. . . . It projects the end of Israel and of Judah, for this was the result of their becoming like the peoples of Canaan. . . .

"This chapter is an end and a beginning. It marks the end of the first generation; it also points to the beginning of a whole new series of wicked acts that will finally lead to Israel's punishment."[13]

18. Summarize the events of chapter 25 regarding the incident with the Moabite woman, the response of Phinehas, and God's commendation of Phinehas.

_____

_____

_____

_____

"The Bible startles its readers by the way it juxtaposes the brightest of revelations and the darkest of sins. . . . Here we have another classic example of this pattern, the wonderful prophecies of Balaam are succeeded by the great apostasy at Peor. In this way Scripture tries to bring home to us the full wonder of God's grace in face of man's incorrigible propensity to sin."[14]

Israel yoked themselves to the Baal of Peor
(25:3). "By participating in this cult Israel had yoked or coupled himself to Baal of Peor. In so doing they flagrantly repudiated the essential heart of the covenant, total and exclusive allegiance to the LORD."[15] Also, we will learn later—in 31:16—that Balaam played a notable part in this.

19. What do God's actions and responses in Numbers 25 demonstrate about His character?

_____

_____

_____

_____

20. What does Numbers 25 demonstrate about the character of Phinehas?

_____

_____

_____

_____

"Since the hero of our story is a priest, our estimation of priests and priesthood should be enhanced. These men could be noble and brave; they are not just cultic functionaries. Then we remember that Christ is priest. He is noble and brave. The best in priests points to Christ. This is true of Aaron, Eleazar, and Phinehas. The chapter celebrates a great priest, just as it excoriates a terrible evil."[16]

"Some Christian commentators have seen Phinehas as a type of Christ. In that he embodied the ideal of Israelite priest-

111

hood this is surely legitimate: our Lord was angry more than once with sin (e.g. Mark 3:5; 11:15ff.). Yet there is another side to it: whereas it was Phinehas' spear that pierced the sinners that made atonement for Israel, it was the nails and spear that pierced Jesus that made atonement for the sins of the whole world."[17]

My covenant of peace with him (25:12). See also God's words in Malachi 2:4-5, which may refer to God's covenant with Phinehas, especially in stating, "he revered me and stood in awe of my name."

---

21. What would you select as the key verse or passage in Numbers 20–25 — one that best captures or reflects the dynamics of what these chapters are all about?

_____

_____

_____

22. List any lingering questions you have about Numbers 20–25.

_____

_____

_____

_____

For the Group

You may want to focus your discussion for lesson 10 on the following issues, themes, and concepts. (These will likely reflect what group members have learned in their individual study of this week's passage, though they'll also have made discoveries in other areas as well.)

- Patience and endurance
- Upholding the holiness of God's name
- Spiritual warfare
- The enduring blessing of God upon His people
- The envisioned future for God's people
- The promise of Messiah

The following numbered questions in lesson 10 may stimulate your best and most helpful discussion: 2, 6, 8, 10, 14, 16, 19, 20, 21, and 22.

Remember to look also at the "For Thought and Discussion" questions in the margin.

1. Ronald B. Allen, "Numbers," in *The Expositor's Bible Commentary*, vol. 2, ed. Frank E. Gaebelein (Grand Rapids, MI: Zondervan, 1990), 866.
2. Allen, 676.
3. *ESV Study Bible* (Wheaton, IL: Crossway, 2008), at Numbers 21:9.
4. Allen, 677.
5. Gordon J. Wenham, "Numbers: An Introduction and Commentary," in the *Tyndale Old Testament Commentaries*, vol. 4, ed. D. J. Wiseman (Downers Grove, IL: InterVarsity, 1981), 185.
6. Wenham, 186.
7. Wenham, 190.
8. Allen, 901.
9. Allen, 904.
10. Allen, 908.
11. *NIV Study Bible* (Grand Rapids, MI: Zondervan, 1985), at Numbers 24:17.
12. Allen, 909.
13. Allen, 914, 916.
14. Wenham, 206.
15. Wenham, 208.
16. Allen, 921.
17. Wenham, 211–212.

NUMBERS 26–30

A New Generation

These are the ones counted . . . on the plains of Moab by the Jordan. . . . Not one of them was among those counted . . . in the Desert of Sinai. For the LORD had told those Israelites they would surely die in the wilderness.

NUMBERS 26:63-65

For Thought and Discussion: Why are fresh starts so psychologically important for us? In what areas of life do they mean the most?

The book of Numbers opened with a census to register the number of fighting-age Israelites among the generation that left Egypt and journeyed to Sinai. Now, in Numbers 26, there is a new census for a new generation.

This new census "develops one of the great themes of the book of Numbers: God's promises to the patriarchs may be delayed by human sin, but they are not ultimately frustrated by it."[1]

1. In what notable ways does the census in chapter 26 compare with that of chapter 1?

   _____

   _____

   _____

   _____

Optional Application: What new beginning has God given you at this time in your life? Thank Him for this, and ask for His help in making the most of your fresh opportunity.

After the plague (26:1). "The plague of chapter 25 was not just another plague; it was the final judgment of God on the first generation and the opportunity to unleash the blessing of God on the second generation who have now reached their majority. . . . It was time for the new generation to be numbered and mustered for the campaign of conquest that now awaited them."[2]

In the census of the first generation (in Numbers 1) and that of the second (in Numbers 26), "the total numbers of the people remain nearly precisely the same. This is an enormous miracle, a great demonstration of the power of God to do his will and work even in the most unlikely of places. But the new generation will also have to face its tests. . . . Is it possible that the new generation will finally be used of God to enter the land, to conquer the inhabitants . . . and to enjoy the land that is God's great and gracious gift for them?"[3]

Israelites who came out of Egypt (26:4). "This generation is regarded as the Exodus people. It is as though their parents had not lived, as though they had not rebelled. The new generation is the substitute for the first. The story begins anew, as though the people had just left bondage in Egypt."[4]

2. What background information to the census is highlighted in 26:63-65, and what is the significance of this?

_____

_____

_____

_____

3. What is significant about the legal situation dealt with in 27:1-11 and how it was resolved?

_____

_____

_____

_____

For Further Study:
How was God's command to Moses in 27:12-14 later fulfilled in Deuteronomy 34:1-6?

"The case of the daughters of Zelophehad . . . shows how many of the laws in the Bible came to be enacted. When a problem arose without previous precedent, it was referred to Moses, who then sought the Lord's direction. The decision then became a precedent for future similar cases (cf. 15:32-36; Leviticus 24:10-23). It seems likely that many of the case laws in the Old Testament originated in a similar way."[5]

4. In what ways might the request of the daughters of Zelophehad be a demonstration of their faith (see 27:3-4)?

_____

_____

_____

5. What do the words of 27:12-14 reveal about Moses and about God?

_____

_____

_____

_____

You disobeyed my command (27:14). This refers back to Moses' (and Aaron's) actions in 20:10-13. Later Moses will say of this incident, "The LORD became angry with me" (Deuteronomy 1:37).

"That even Moses would come under the wrath of God is stunning! . . .

"The fourth book of the Pentateuch thus presents a sobering, chilling reality. The God who had entered into covenant with Abraham (Genesis 12), who had delivered his people from bondage in the Exodus (Exodus 14–15), who had revealed his holiness and the means to approach his grace through celebrative and sacrificial worship (Leviticus 1–7) — this same Yahweh was also a God of wrath and a consuming fire. His wrath extends to his errant children as well as to the enemy nations of Egypt and Canaan."[6]

6. a. In 27:15-21, how do Moses and God envision Joshua's leadership?

_____

_____

_____

   b. In what ways do you see this as a model for leadership among God's people today?

_____

_____

_____

God who gives breath to all living things (27:16).
This phrase is used elsewhere only in the prayer
of Moses and Aaron after Korah's rebellion (see
16:22). Here Moses uses it after being reminded
of his coming death, and he prays for God to
provide a new leader for Israel who will be a
spiritual shepherd. "God, as the giver of all life,
must be specially concerned with the continued existence of his chosen people, Israel."[7]

Like sheep without a shepherd (27:17). See also
1 Kings 22:17, Ezekiel 34:5, and Matthew 9:36.

7. From what you see in 27:16-23 and from earlier
in Numbers, how was Joshua uniquely qualified
for the leadership position God was giving him?

_____

_____

_____

_____

8. According to 27:18-23, how will Joshua's leadership differ from that of Moses? In particular,
summarize how the authority Moses has had
will in the future be shared between Joshua and
Eleazar (see verses 20-21).

_____

_____

_____

_____

9. From what you see in Numbers 27:16-18, how is
Joshua a picture of Christ?

_____

_____

_____

_____

For Further Study:
What do you learn about Joshua's past in Exodus 17:9-14, 24:13, 32:17, and 33:11?

For Further Study:
How do you see the growing confirmation and acceptance of Joshua's leadership as indicated in Deuteronomy 31:14-15,23; Joshua 1:1-9; 4:13-14; and 5:13-15?

Joshua . . . a man in whom is the spirit (27:18); or *a man in whom is the Spirit* (NIV marginal reading). "The term 'spirit' can refer to his own leadership capacity, as would be suggested by the NIV's lower-case reading; perhaps 'the spirit [of leadership]' is intended. But it is also possible, as the NIV margin has it, to read the word 'Spirit' as a distinct reference to the Holy Spirit. This latter seems to be more likely. . . . It is possible that this phrase means that Joshua was Spirit-endowed as the leader of the people (see Deuteronomy 34:9: 'Joshua son of Nun was filled with the spirit of wisdom'), phrasing that is hauntingly suggested of New Testament language concerning the Spirit of God (see Acts 6:5)."[8] See also Genesis 41:38; Judges 3:10.

Lay your hand on him (27:18). See also Numbers 27:23; Deuteronomy 34:9. "Despite the difference in authority between Moses and Joshua, there was a real continuity between them expressed symbolically by the laying on of Moses' hands. In this symbolic gesture Joshua was identified with Moses and made his representative for the future."[9] For this practice in the New Testament, see Acts 6:6; 13:3; 1 Timothy 4:14; Hebrews 6:2.

10. As attention is drawn again in chapters 28–29 to Israel's sacrificial offerings in her relationship to the Lord, what significance do you see in this emphasis?

_____

_____

_____

_____

"Although Moses' days as mediator of revelation are numbered, he still is God's chosen vessel to pass on law to Israel. First among his final instructions are laws about public sacrifices [see also Exodus

23:10-19; 34:18-26; Leviticus 23; Deuteronomy 16:1-17]. . . . These regulations make
several points.

"First, they show the importance
of the sacrificial system in Israel. In the
limited time before his death, Moses
explains what sacrifices must be offered
in public worship on behalf of the whole
nation. These are over and above the private sacrifices that a layperson may want
to bring for personal reasons.

"Second, they are a strong assurance
to Joshua that the nation will indeed
inherit the land and become a pros-
perous agricultural community, able
to provide for this lavish and expensive
worship. . . .

"Finally, this list of sacrifices under-
lines the importance of the sabbatical
principle. Every seventh day is a Sabbath
and marked by a doubling of the daily
sacrifice, while the seventh month is
marked by a huge number of extra
sacrifices, especially during the Feast of
Booths, which is clearly marked out as
the biggest celebration of the year."[10]

Optional Application: In what ways are the regula-tions for daily offer-ings (see 28:1-8) to be a model for your own daily worship of the Lord?

11. From 28:1-8, summarize the regulations given
    for daily offerings.

    _____

    _____

    _____

    _____

    _____

12. From 28:9-10, summarize the regulations given for Sabbath offerings.

_____

_____

_____

13. From 28:11-15, summarize the regulations given for monthly offerings.

_____

_____

_____

14. From 28:16-25, summarize the regulations given for Passover offerings.

_____

_____

_____

15. From 28:26-31, summarize the regulations given regarding offerings for the Feast of Weeks.

_____

_____

_____

16. From 29:1-6, summarize the regulations given regarding offerings for the Feast of Trumpets.

_____

_____

_____

17. From 29:7-11, summarize the regulations given regarding offerings for the Day of Atonement.

_____

_____

_____

18. From 29:12-40, summarize the regulations given regarding offerings for the Feast of Tabernacles (or "Feast of Booths," ESV).

_____

_____

_____

"The New Testament views all the old covenant sacrifices as types of the death of Christ. The different sacrifices bring out different aspects of the significance of his death. Lambs sacrificed every morning and evening were the most typical victim, so Jesus is called 'the Lamb of God, who takes away the sin of the world' (John 1:29). Indeed, he died at the time of the evening sacrifice. His death made animal sacrifice obsolete. . . .

"But Jewish and Christian commentators have always regarded the daily burnt offerings as a model of worship for all time. Prayer should be offered at least every morning and evening: indeed, the whole of life is to be dedicated to God through repeated acts of praise and thanksgiving (cf. Romans 12:1; 1 Thessalonians 5:16-18)."[11]

19. What is significant in the regulations for vows given in chapter 30?

_____

_____

_____

_____

20. What would you select as the key verse or passage in Numbers 26–30 — one that best captures or reflects the dynamics of what these chapters are all about?

_____

_____

_____

21. List any lingering questions you have about Numbers 26–30.

_____

_____

_____

_____

For the Group

You may want to focus your discussion for lesson 11 especially on the following issues, themes, and concepts. (These will likely reflect what group members have learned in their individual study of this week's passage, though they'll also have made discoveries in other areas as well.)

- New beginnings for God's people
- Appropriate leadership for God's people
- Appropriate worship of God and celebration by His people
- Commitment in our vows made to the Lord

The following numbered questions in lesson 11 may stimulate your best and most helpful discussion: 2, 4, 5, 6, 9, 10, 20, and 21.

Remember to look also at the "For Thought and Discussion" questions in the margin.

1. Gordon J. Wenham, "Numbers: An Introduction and Commentary," in the *Tyndale Old Testament Commentaries*, vol. 4, ed. D. J. Wiseman (Downers Grove, IL: InterVarsity, 1981), 213.

2. Ronald B. Allen, "Numbers," in *The Expositor's Bible Commentary*, vol. 2, ed. Frank E. Gaebelein (Grand Rapids, MI: Zondervan, 1990), 925.
3. Allen, 924.
4. Allen, 926.
5. Wenham, 215.
6. Allen, 676.
7. Wenham, 217.
8. Allen, 946.
9. Wenham, 218.
10. *ESV Study Bible* (Wheaton, IL: Crossway, 2008), at Numbers 28–29.
11. Wenham, 223.

NUMBERS 31–36

Preparing for Canaan

When you cross the Jordan into Canaan, drive out all the inhabitants of the land before you. Destroy all their carved images and their cast idols, and demolish all their high places. Take possession of the land and settle in it, for I have given you the land to possess.

NUMBERS 33:51-53

1. From chapter 31, summarize what happens — and why — in Israel's conflict with the Midianites.

   _____

   _____

   _____

   _____

2. In 31:13-18, what is significant about how Moses' anger was incited and how he responded?

   _____

   _____

   _____

3. What additional perspective do we gain about Balaam in 31:16?

127

_____

_____

_____

In the Peor incident (31:16). See Numbers 25.

4. Reviewing chapter 31, what do we learn about the way the Lord does battle against His people's enemies?

_____

_____

_____

_____

The lands of Jazer and Gilead (32:1). These are the regions once ruled by Sihon and Og, the kings defeated by Israel in Numbers 21.

5. From chapter 32, summarize the issue that caused Moses to be upset and how it was resolved.

_____

_____

_____

_____

6. What is significant about the way the itinerary in chapter 33 is introduced (see verses 1-4)?

_____

_____

_____

7. What important information do we discover in the special notation inserted in the itinerary at 33:38-39?

_____

_____

_____

For Thought and Discussion: What benefits might the later generations of Israel derive from reviewing Moses' journey summary in Numbers 33?

8. What is the significance of the warnings given in 33:50-56, especially at this stage in Israel's journey?

_____

_____

_____

_____

9. What significance do you see in the boundary information given in chapter 34?

_____

_____

_____

_____

10. From chapter 35, summarize the information (and its significance) regarding the cities for the Levites and the cities of refuge.

_____

_____

_____

_____

Bloodshed pollutes the land (35:33). "The crime of murder is not only an offense against the sanctity of life; it is in fact a pollutant to the Lord's sacred land."[1]

"Canaan is more than the promised land: it is the holy land sanctified by the presence of God living among his people (35:34; cf. Leviticus 26:11-12). It is therefore of the utmost importance to keep this land pure especially from the most potent pollution of shed blood. It is paradoxical that in the right place blood is the most effective purifier, the only means of atonement between God and man, but in the wrong context it has precisely the opposite effect."[2]

11. What further developments are given in chapter 36 regarding the issue that arose in 27:1-11?

_____

_____

_____

_____

"There is hope in the actions of the daughters of Zelophehad that they will be representative of the nation: this generation will do well."[3]

Every Israelite shall keep the tribal inheritance of their ancestors (36:7). "Formally this is of course a statement of a legal principle . . . but theologically, like many of the laws in Numbers, it is a promise that the tribes of Israel will always dwell in their God-given land. . . . On this strong note of hope the book closes, inviting the curious to read on to see how God's purposes were worked out in the subsequent history of Israel."[4]

---

12. As the book of Numbers concludes, what would you say are the greatest challenges or potential dangers facing the people of Israel at this time?

_____

_____

_____

_____

13. What would you select as the key verse or passage in Numbers 31–36—one that best captures or reflects the dynamics of what these chapters are all about?

_____

_____

_____

14. List any lingering questions you have about Numbers 31–36.

_____

_____

_____

_____

Reviewing Numbers

15. Consider again God's reminder in Isaiah 55:10-11—that in the same way He sends rain and snow from the sky to water the earth and nurture life, so also He sends His words to accomplish specific purposes. What would you suggest are God's primary purposes for the message of Numbers in the lives of His people today?

_____

_____

_____

_____

For Further Study: In 1 Corinthians 10:1-14, notice how Paul refers to various events in Numbers (as well as in Exodus and Leviticus) and states, "These things happened to them as examples and were written down as warnings for us" (10:11). Look over 1 Corinthians 10 as you recall the various events in Numbers that Paul alludes to. What are the most important warnings these things should have for us?

Optional Application: In light of Paul's words in 1 Corinthians 10:1-14, what personal warnings from the book of Numbers do you believe *you* need most to take to heart?

"For the writers of the New Testament the book of Numbers stands as a great warning. Despite the miraculous deliverance from Egypt, and the daily evidences of God's provision for their needs, Israel refused to believe and rebelled against their Savior. Numbers records a trial of spectacular judgments that ought to provoke caution in every believer."[5]

16. Recall once again the guidelines given for our thought life in Philippians 4:8: "Whatever is true, whatever is noble, whatever is right, whatever is pure, whatever is lovely, whatever is admirable — if anything is excellent or praiseworthy — *think about such things*" (emphasis added). As you reflect on all you've read in the book of Numbers, what stands out to you as being particularly *true, noble, right, pure, lovely, admirable, excellent,* or *praiseworthy* — and therefore well worth thinking more about?

_____

_____

_____

_____

17. Since all of Scripture testifies ultimately of Christ, where does *Jesus* come most in focus for you in this book?

_____

_____

_____

_____

18. What are the strongest ways in which Numbers points us to mankind's need for Jesus and to what He accomplished in His death and resurrection?

_____

_____

_____

_____

19. Recall again Paul's reminder that the Old Testament Scriptures can give us patience and perseverance on one hand, as well as comfort and encouragement on the other (see Romans 15:4). In your own life, how do you see the book of Numbers living up to Paul's description? In what ways does it help to meet your personal needs for both perseverance and encouragement?

_____

_____

_____

_____

20. What is the best evidence you've seen in Numbers that God truly loves His people?

_____

_____

_____

_____

21. Since the Bible is our ultimate handbook for worship and service, what is the best help you see in the book of Numbers for strengthening our worship of God and our service to others?

_____

_____

_____

Optional Application: Which verses in Numbers would be most helpful for you to memorize, so you have them always available in your mind and heart for the Holy Spirit to use?

For Further Study: How does Psalm 78:5-8 reflect the ultimate meaning and message of the book of Numbers?

For the Group

You may want to focus your discussion for lesson 12 especially on the following issues, themes, and concepts. (These will likely reflect what group members have learned in their individual study of this week's passage, though they'll also have made discoveries in other areas as well.)

- Envisioning and planning for our future as God's people
- Spiritual warfare
- God's faithfulness in leading His people

The following numbered questions in lesson 12 may stimulate your best and most helpful discussion: 1, 2, 4, 6, 8, 12, 13, and 14.

Allow enough discussion time to look back together and review all of Numbers as a whole. You can use questions 15–21 in this lesson to help you do that.

Once more, look also at the questions in the margin under the heading "For Thought and Discussion."

1. Ronald B. Allen, "Numbers," in *The Expositor's Bible Commentary*, vol. 2, ed. Frank E. Gaebelein (Grand Rapids, MI: Zondervan, 1990), 1005.
2. Gordon J. Wenham, "Numbers: An Introduction and Commentary," in the *Tyndale Old Testament Commentaries*, vol. 4, ed. D. J. Wiseman (Downers Grove, IL: InterVarsity, 1981), 262.
3. Allen, 1008.
4. Wenham, 267.
5. Wenham, 56.

STUDY AIDS

For further information on the material in this study, consider the following sources. They are available on the Internet (www.christianbook.com, www .amazon.com, and so on), or your local Christian bookstore should be able to order any of them if it does not carry them. Most seminary libraries have them, as well as many university and public libraries. If they are out of print, you might be able to find them online.

Commentaries on Leviticus

R. Laird Harris, "Leviticus," in *The Expositor's Bible Commentary*, vol. 2 (Zondervan, 1990).

John E. Hartley, *Leviticus*, vol. 4 of *Word Biblical Commentary* (Thomas Nelson, 1992).

Jacob Milgrom, *Leviticus*, Continental Commentary (Augsberg, 2004).

Mark F. Rooker, *Leviticus*, vol. 3A of *The New American Commentary* (Broadman & Holman, 2000).

Gordon J. Wenham, *The Book of Leviticus*, New International Commentary on the Old Testament (Eerdmans, 1979).

Commentaries on Numbers

Ronald B. Allen, "Numbers," in *The Expositor's Bible Commentary*, vol. 2 (Zondervan, 1990).

Timothy R. Ashley, *The Book of Numbers*, New International Commentary on the Old Testament (Eerdmans, 1993).

R. Dennis Cole, *Numbers*, vol. 3B of *The New American Commentary* (Broadman & Holman, 2000).

Iain M. Duguid, *Numbers: God's Presence in the Wilderness*, Preaching the Word (Crossway, 2006).

Gordon J. Wenham, *Numbers: An Introduction and Commentary*, Tyndale Old Testament Commentaries (InterVarsity, 1981).

Historical background sources and handbooks

Bible study becomes more meaningful when modern Western readers understand the times and places in which the biblical authors lived. *The IVP Bible Background Commentary: Old Testament,* by John H. Walton, Victor H. Matthews, and Mark W. Chavalas (InterVarsity, 2000), provides insight into the ancient Near Eastern world, its peoples, customs, and geography to help contemporary readers better understand the context in which the Old Testament Scriptures were written.

A **handbook** of biblical customs can also be useful. Some good ones are the time-proven updated classic *Halley's Bible Handbook with the New International Version,* by Henry H. Halley (Zondervan, 2007), and the inexpensive paperback *Manners and Customs in the Bible,* by Victor H. Matthews (Hendrickson, 1991).

Concordances, dictionaries, and encyclopedias

A **concordance** lists words of the Bible alphabetically along with each verse in which the word appears. It lets you do your own word studies. An *exhaustive* concordance lists every word used in a given translation, while an *abridged* or *complete* concordance omits either some words, some occurrences of the word, or both.

Two of the best exhaustive concordances are *Strong's Exhaustive Concordance* and *The Strongest NIV Exhaustive Concordance. Strong's* is available based on the King James Version of the Bible and the New American Standard Bible. *Strong's* has an index by which you can find out which Greek or Hebrew word is used in a given English verse. The NIV concordance does the same thing except it also includes an index for Aramaic words in the original texts from which the NIV was translated. However, neither concordance requires knowledge of the original languages. *Strong's* is available online at www.biblestudytools.com. Both are also available in hard copy.

A **Bible dictionary** or **Bible encyclopedia** alphabetically lists articles about people, places, doctrines, important words, customs, and geography of the Bible.

Holman Illustrated Bible Dictionary, by C. Brand, C. W. Draper, and A. England (B&H, 2003), offers more than seven hundred color photos, illustrations, and charts; sixty full-color maps; and up-to-date archaeological findings, along with exhaustive definitions of people, places, things, and events—dealing with every subject in the Bible. It uses a variety of Bible translations and is the only dictionary that includes the ESV, HCSB, KJV, NASB, NIV, NRSV, REB, RSV, and TEV.

The New Unger's Bible Dictionary, Revised and Expanded, by Merrill F. Unger (Moody, 2006), has been a best seller for almost fifty years. Its 6,700-plus entries reflect the most current scholarship and more than 1,200,000 words are supplemented with detailed essays, colorful photography and maps, and dozens of charts and illustrations to enhance your understanding of God's Word. Based on the New American Standard Bible.

The Zondervan Encyclopedia of the Bible, edited by Moisés Silva and Merrill C. Tenney (Zondervan, 2008), is excellent and exhaustive. However, its five 1,000-page volumes are a financial investment, so all but very serious students may prefer to use it at a church, public, college, or seminary library.

Unlike a Bible dictionary in the above sense, *Vine's Complete Expository Dictionary of Old and New Testament Words,* by W. E. Vine, Merrill F. Unger, and William White Jr. (Thomas Nelson, 1996), alphabetically lists major words used in the King James Version and defines each Old Testament Hebrew or New Testament Greek word the KJV translates with that English word. *Vine's* lists verse references where that Hebrew or Greek word appears so that you can do your own cross-references and word studies without knowing the original languages.

The Brown-Driver-Briggs Hebrew and English Lexicon by Francis Brown, C. Briggs, and S. R. Driver (Hendrickson, 1996), is probably the most respected and comprehensive Bible lexicon for Old Testament studies. *BDB* gives not only dictionary definitions for each word but relates each word to its Old Testament usage and categorizes its nuances of meaning.

Bible atlases and map books

A **Bible atlas** can be a great aid to understanding what is going on in a book of the Bible and how geography affected events. Here are a few good choices:

The Hammond Atlas of Bible Lands (Langenscheidt, 2007) packs a ton of resources into just sixty-four pages. Maps, of course, but also photographs, illustrations, and a comprehensive timeline. You'll find an introduction to the unique geography of the Holy Land, including terrain, trade routes, vegetation, and climate information.

The New Moody Atlas of the Bible, by Barry J. Beitzel (Moody, 2009), is scholarly, very evangelical, and full of theological text, indexes, and references. Beitzel shows vividly how God prepared the land of Israel perfectly for the acts of salvation He was going to accomplish in it.

Then and Now Bible Maps Insert (Rose, 2008) is a nifty paperback that is sized just right to fit inside your Bible cover. Only forty-four pages long, it features clear plastic overlays of modern-day cities and countries so you can see what nation or city now occupies the Bible setting you are reading about. Every major city of the Bible is included.

For small-group leaders

Discipleship Journal's Best Small-Group Ideas, Volumes 1 and 2 (NavPress, 2005). Each volume is packed with 101 of the best hands-on tips and group-building principles from *Discipleship Journal's* "Small Group Letter" and "DJ Plus" as well as articles from the magazine. They will help you inject new passion into the life of your small group.

Bill Donahue, *Leading Life-Changing Small Groups* (Zondervan, 2002). This comprehensive resource is packed with information, practical tips, and insights that will teach you about small-group philosophy and structure, discipleship, conducting meetings, and more.

Neal F. McBride, *How to Build a Small-Groups Ministry* (NavPress, 1994). *How to Build a Small-Groups Ministry* is a time-proven, hands-on workbook for pastors and lay leaders that includes everything you need to know to develop a plan that fits your unique church. Through basic principles, case studies, and worksheets, McBride leads you through twelve logical steps for organizing and administering a small-groups ministry.

Neal F. McBride, *How to Lead Small Groups* (NavPress, 1990). This book covers leadership skills for all kinds of small groups: Bible study, fellowship, task, and support groups. Filled with step-by-step guidance and practical exercises to help you grasp the critical aspects of small-group leadership and dynamics.

Tara Miller and Jenn Peppers, *Finding the Flow: A Guide for Leading Small Groups and Gatherings* (IVP Connect, 2008). *Finding the Flow* offers a fresh take on leading small groups by seeking to develop the leader's small-group facilitation skills.

Bible study methods

Discipleship Journal's Best Bible Study Methods (NavPress, 2002). This is a collection of thirty-two creative ways to explore Scripture that will help you enjoy studying God's Word more.

Howard Hendricks and William Hendricks, *Living by the Book: The Art and Science of Reading the Bible* (Moody, 2007). *Living by the Book* offers a practical three-step process to help you master simple yet effective inductive methods of observation, interpretation, and application that will make all the difference in your time with God's Word. A workbook by the same title is also available to go along with the book.

The Navigator Bible Studies Handbook (NavPress, 1994). This resource teaches the underlying principles for doing good inductive Bible study, including instructions on doing queston-and-answer studies, verse-analysis studies, chapter-analysis studies, and topical studies.

Rick Warren, *Rick Warren's Bible Study Methods: Twelve Ways You Can Unlock God's Word* (Zondervan, 2006). Rick Warren offers simple, step-by-step instructions, guiding you through twelve different approaches to studying the Bible for yourself with the goal of becoming more like Jesus.

Discover What
the Bible Really Says

LifeChange by The Navigators

The LifeChange Bible study series can help you grow in Christlikeness through a life-changing encounter with God's Word. Discover what the Bible says—not what someone else thinks it says—and develop the skills and desire to dig even deeper into God's Word. Each study includes study aids and discussion questions.

The Message Means Understanding

Bringing the Bible to all ages

The Message is written in contemporary language that is much like talking with a good friend. When paired with your favorite Bible study, *The Message* will deliver a reading experience that is reliable, energetic, and amazingly fresh.